Ellen Lupton

COOPER-HEWITT

NATIONAL MUSEUM OF DESIGN

SMITHSONIAN INSTITUTION

PRINCETON

ARCHITECTURAL

PRESS

WOMEN AND MACHINES FROM HOME TO OFFICE

Published by Cooper-Hewitt
National Museum of Design
Smithsonian Institution
and Princeton Architectural Press.

Cooper-Hewitt
National Museum of Design
Smithsonian Institution
2 East 91st Street
New York, New York 10128

Princeton Architectural Press
37 East 7th Street
New York, New York 10003

The paper used in this publication meets the minimum requirements of the American National Standard for Permanence of Paper for Printed Library Materials, ANSI Z39.48-1984

COVER PHOTO (LEFT), ad for AT&T kitchen phone, late 1950s.
COVER PHOTO (RIGHT), telephone operators, New York, Schomburg Center, New York Public Library.
INSIDE COVER PHOTO, a government secretary cleaning her typewriter, 1943. Marjory Collins, Library of Congress.

LIBRARY OF CONGRESS
CATALOGING-IN-PUBLICATION DATA
Lupton, Ellen.
Mechanical brides: women and machines
from home to office / Ellen Lupton.
p. cm.
Published to accompany an exhibition
of the same name, to be held at Cooper-
Hewitt from 8-17-93 to 1-4-94.
Includes bibliographic references.
ISBN 1-878271-97-0
1. Women—United States—Social
conditions. 2. Technology—Social
aspects—United States. 3. Household
appliances—Social aspects—United
States. 4. Office equipment and
supplies—Social aspects—United States.
5. Sex role—United States. 6. Design,
Industrial—United States—Social aspects.
I. Cooper-Hewitt Museum. II. Title.
HQ1420.L87 1993
305.42'0973—dc20 93-22169
CIP

EDITING
Nancy Aakre, Maud Lavin,
Susan Yelavich

BOOK DESIGN
Ellen Lupton and Hall Smyth

COVER DESIGN
J. Abbott Miller and Hall Smyth

PHOTO CREDITS

COVER, telephone operators, photo also appears on PAGE 32. Photographs and Prints Division, Schomburg Center for Research in Black Culture, New York Public Library, Astor, Lenox & Tilden Foundations.

PAGE 12, *Wizard of Oz* appliances, photos by Kevin Piasceczny.

PAGE 18, *The Incredible Shrinking Woman*, © Universal City Studios, Inc. Courtesy of MCA Publishing Rights, a division of MCA, Inc.

PAGE 24, Mrs. Potts's iron, The New-York Historical Society, New York.

PAGE 25, photos of irons, by Ken Pelka.

PAGE 41, Pepsi ad reproduced with permission of PepsiCo, Inc., 1993, Purchase, New York. Donna Karan ad, courtesy The Donna Karan Company, © DK Co., 1993.

PAGE 35, secretary with 500 set, courtesy Listerine.

PAGE 45, Corry Jamestown file cabinets, courtesy Corry Hiebert, a Hon Industries Corporation.

PAGES 46–47, Royal typewriters, Royal Consumer Business Products, a division of Olivetti Office USA. IBM typewriters, courtesy IBM Corporation.

PAGE 49, Western Union facsimile machine, courtesy New Valley Corp.

PAGE 53, *The Desk Set*, © 1957, Twentieth Century Fox Film Corporation. All rights reserved.

PAGE 54, ads for *Charm*, from the collection of the Center for Advertising History, National Museum of American Art, Smithsonian Institution. Courtesy Condé Nast Publishing, Inc.

Printed in Hong Kong

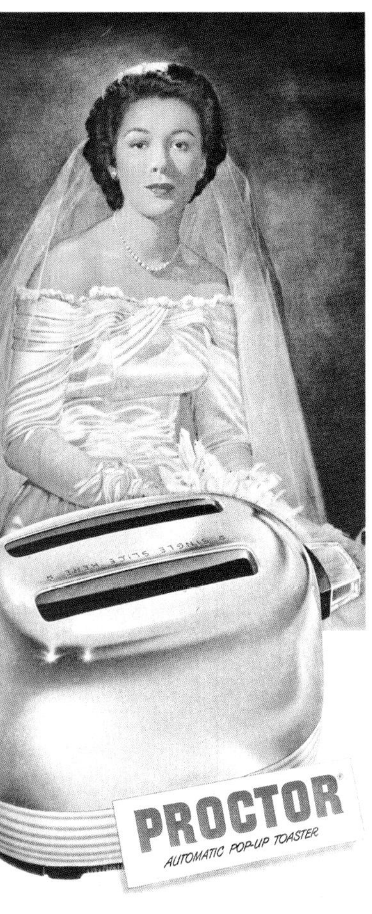

1949. Courtesy Hamilton Beach/ Proctor-Silex, Inc.

CONTENTS

FOREWORD

Dianne H. Pilgrim, Director

As the National Museum of Design, Cooper-Hewitt explores how design affects every aspect of our daily lives by encouraging people to think in new ways about the creation and consequences of the built environment. One area for study is the *uses* people make of designed objects, from their practical function to their role in crafting cultural identities and hierarchies.

This publication and the exhibition that it accompanies, *Mechanical Brides: Women and Machines from Home to Office,* looks at the central place of laundry equipment, telephones, and typewriters in the cultural differences between women and men in American life. Assumptions about the aspirations and responsibilities of women are reflected and reinforced by the ways these machines have been designed, marketed, used, and imagined in the twentieth century. *Mechanical Brides* looks at the gender significance of seemingly neutral things by viewing them from the perspective of female consumers and users.

Cooper-Hewitt, National Museum of Design, is indebted to the NYNEX family of companies for their generous support of this project, and for their collaboration in designing the interactive telephone installations featured in the exhibition. We also thank Smithsonian Institution's Special Exhibition Fund for its generous grant. Additional suppport was provided by Helen Hunt and The Sister Fund, and by Margaret Schink. I thank Sheri Sandler for her passionate belief that this project should be funded in part by feminists who are committed to the empowerment of women at a grass roots level.

In May 1992 Ellen Lupton accepted the newly created position of Curator of Contemporary Design. During her short tenure she has already contributed significantly to the mission of the Museum. *Mechanical Brides: Women and Machines from Home to Office* illustrates her many abilities: a keen intellect, a great knowledge and understanding of design, and an ability to express her ideas, both verbally and graphically, with clarity and insight. I thank Ellen for looking at design and its relationship to society in a fresh and innovative way.

This 1948 Clorox ad compares housekeeping to the work performed in a museum; both involve the loving care of objects.

ACKNOWLEDGMENTS

Several strong women stand behind this project. My mother, Mary Jane Lupton, taught me to be a feminist through her work as a writer, teacher, activist, and parent. My mother-in-law, Ruby Miller (1933-1993), demonstrated the heroism of women's lives through the complexity and fullness of her own. Dianne H. Pilgrim contributed enormously to the study of design with the 1986 exhibition and book *The Machine Age in America*; I thank her for supporting my work at Cooper-Hewitt, National Museum of Design, Smithsonian Institution.

Other friends and family members have helped me through this project, including J. Abbott Miller, Julia Reinhard Lupton, Kenneth Baldwin, William and Shirley Lupton, Kenneth Reinhard, and Jennifer Tobias.

This project depended on the creativity and stamina of Sheri Sandler, who located, documented, and selected the three-dimensional artifacts featured in the exhibition. As editorial advisors, Nancy Aakre, Maud Lavin, and Susan Yelavich kept the texts of the book and exhibition focused and direct. Hall Smyth worked on the book's design and production, and Alisa Grifo managed film and photography research for the book and exhibition. John Fell, Betsy Roxby, Laurene Leon, and Constantin Boym directed the design and installation of the exhibition. Mark Avnet and Sharleen Smith worked with NYNEX Science and Technology to design the interactive phone installations. Deirdre Scott directed the oral history project. Dorothy Dunn, Kerry MacIntosh, Egle Zygas, and Laurie McGavin Bachmann orchestrated ambitious educational programs. Cathleen Campbell produced the laundry video. Laura James led the development campaign. Crucial advocacy and useful criticism were provided at the project's earliest stages by Andrew Pekarik.

Many other colleagues at Cooper-Hewitt contributed ideas and energy, including James Elliott Benjamin, Daniel Billy, Bridget Calzaretta, David Carr, Gail Davidson, Nicholas Dileo, Florence Duhl, Linda Dunne, Hank Edelman, Russell Flinchum, Laura Ford, Dorothy Globus, Matt Hahn, Peter Hildebrand, Florence Lewis, Gwen Loeffler, David Revere McFadden, Christine McKee, Christine Moctezuma, Caroline Mortimer, Gillian Moss, Margie Neuhaus, Brad Nugent, Phoebe Prentice, John Richardson, Belynda Roebuck, Sarane Ross, Brent Rumage, Danielle Schwartz, Raul Serrano, Camille She, Deborah Shinn, Jim Stubenrauch, Marilyn Symmes, Rachel Switzky, Stephen Van Dyk, Joanne Warner, Mathew Weaver, Leonard Webers, Ellisa Whitely, and Alex Zane.

1942. Courtesy Hamilton Beach/ Proctor-Silex, Inc.

Colleagues from other Smithsonian bureaus and outside institutions have offered valuable help, including Kimberly Barta, Cathy Brawer, Gordon Christmas, Zahava Doering, Estelle Ellis, Stuart Ewen, Helen Federico, John Fleckner, Ian Gordon, Robert Hardie, Claudia Kidwell, Kevin Lippert, Susan Grant Lewin, Elizabeth Marcus, Frances McDonald, Chee Pearlman, Rodris Roth, Fath Ruffins, Barbara Schneider, Elliot Sivowitch, Claudia Stagg, Carlene Stevens, Sally Stein, Catherine Hoover Voorsanger, Kay Youngflesh, Hillary Weiss, and Geraldine Wu.

Lenders to the exhibition include Linda Bower/Telephenomenal, Marjorie Chester, Vincent Cracchiolo, Hobart van Deusen, Charles Diehl, Frogdesign, Marilyn Gabor/ Moderne Antiques, Mr. and Mrs. Gerald Gapa, Joseph Holtzman, Marshall Johnson, Carole Krohn, H. L. Kupper, John Lefever, Paul Lippman, Kate Loye, Larry Salomon, Barbara Owen-Smithen, Richard Prelinger, Andy Rooney, Jacqueline Ruhl, Seiko Telecommunications Systems, Inc., Alex Shear/The Nostalgia Brokers, Wesley Smith, Ronald Schaffer, Donald Sutherland, Harvey Stuart/The Fonebooth, Tom Stiyer, Peter Tytell, Gerhard Winkler, and Donald Wilkes. Corporate collections were made available to us by Hamilton Beach/Proctor-Silex, Inc., Maytag Co., and AT&T Archives. The American Advertising Museum, the Chinatown History Museum, the National Museum of American History, the Metropolitan Museum of Art, and the Maidenform Museum also participated as lenders to the exhibition. E. L.

TOASTIMONIAL

Our "Toastmaster" toaster was a wedding gift eight years ago. It's still as bright as new, and has been popping up wonderful toast nearly every day for all these years. Thank you for so much perfection.

ELEANOR AND ALBERT JACKSON
Duluth, Minn.

Something old . . . something new

This treasured gift of generations of fortunate brides is new in beauty and performance . . . *but old in experience.* A quarter-century of pioneering and perfecting the art of automatic toasting is woven into this masterpiece of 1946. So be sure of this—a "*Toastmaster*"* toaster is the one she will want. And she will happily remember you for it, through years of blissful breakfasts. . . . If your dealer hasn't it now, he'll gladly take your order—and do his best to deliver. Our production is steadily mounting, but the *demand* is still far ahead of us.

TOASTMASTER *Automatic Pop-Up Toasters*

*"TOASTMASTER" is a registered trademark of McGraw Electric Company, manufacturers of Buss Electric Fuses, Clark Electric Water Heaters, and Toastmaster Products. Copr. 1946, TOASTMASTER PRODUCTS DIVISION, McGraw Electric Company, Elgin, Ill.

RETAILERS: A handsome mounted reprint of this page will be mailed free upon request.

SEX *Objects*

The sexual division of labor is a central feature of the modern home and office. Certain tasks, accomplished with certain tools, have become associated with "women's work," while others traditionally have been assigned to men. Mechanical devices, from the washing machine to the typewriter, are designed to perform work; the work they do is cultural as well as utilitarian, helping to define the differences between women and men.

Human personalities are shaped by social conditions, from ideals of family life and norms of gender behavior to the economic opportunities available to people based on their cultural identities. The self is, to some degree, a manufactured object, a social product. Over the past two centuries, people increasingly have defined themselves through the products they buy and use. The American "standard of living," which rose dramatically in the 1920s and the 1950s, is embodied in an endless inventory of objects. Married women, as the chief purchasing agents for the typical family unit, have been the main targets for many consumer products, from domestic appliances and cleaning products to ready-made clothing and industrially processed foods.

Manufactured goods are connected intimately to the minds and bodies that use them. Through industrial design, marketing campaigns, and the narratives of popular entertainment, useful things perform functions beyond mere utility. As objects of emotional attachment, mechanical devices animate the scenes of daily life, stimulating feelings of love, possibility, and connection, as well as guilt, restriction, and isolation. The self emerges out of material things, which appear to take on lives of their own.

ABOVE *This photo is from a 1938 GE ad for a line of refrigerators designed by Henry Dreyfuss. In the 1930s, the electric refrigerator was a new appliance that few young women would have known in their mothers' homes.*

LEFT *The mirrored surface of a Toastmaster promises a lifetime of blissful breakfasts to the young bride and her husband, 1946. Domestic appliances have been considered ideal bridal gifts since the 1930s, a period when middle-class women could no longer assume they would be able to hire servants. Household machines, no longer kept hidden away in service areas, became part of the public decor of the home.*

As a feminist study of design, this publication looks critically at the values that distinguish the experiences of women and men. Every history has a bias; by calling oneself a feminist, an author names the position from which her story will be told. Accounts of design that claim to speak in a neutral voice tend to center, by default, on male designers, inventors, entrepreneurs, and other *producers* of culture. Women, as the buyers and users of numerous consumer products, are a crucial field against which to view modern design. The concept of "woman" addressed by design and advertising consists of cultural fantasies as well as demographic facts; it encompasses idealized media Moms and eternally sexy secretaries as well as the concrete diversity of the marketplace.

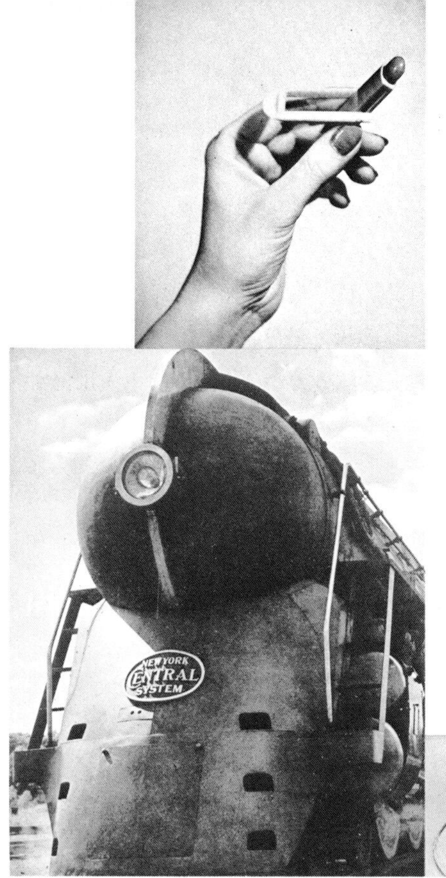

ABOVE LEFT *These two photographs are from J. Gordon Lippincott's 1947 book* Design for Business. *The author juxtaposed these discordant images to invoke the vast range of the designer's vision, which encompasses everything "from lipsticks to locomotives." Ultimately, the emphasis in Lippincott's text falls on products for the intimate world of the female consumer, not the masculine realm of heavy industry.*

ABOVE RIGHT *Domestic love is reflected on the surface of a Coffeemaster automatic coffee maker, 1950. Sunbeam Corporation.*

America's consumer economy gathered force during the nineteenth century. By the 1880s, many urban and suburban families were buying factory-produced clothing, food, furniture, housewares, and other goods that once had been made at home. While men commonly left the house to work for wages, their wives became responsible for buying, using, cleaning, and maintaining consumer goods. Advertising made women its primary object of address, as did modern industrial design, which emerged out of the advertising business in the late 1920s.[1]

From the 1930s through the 1950s, industrial designers applied the aerodynamic styling of trains and planes to home appliances, office machines, and other immobile objects, transforming them into emotionally appealing commodities. By concealing the moving parts of machines inside smooth skins, designers made appliances easier to clean by female users, who have served as the chief custodians of modern standards of hygiene. J. Gordon Lippincott, one of the pioneers of the industrial design profession, claimed in 1947 that since 90 percent of consumers were women, male designers and manufacturers must learn to speak to them.[2]

"If hard-headed business men [could] build up...the cosmetic industry in a few years, and do it on sheer emotional appeal to the American woman, there is no reason why such common everyday objects as alarm clocks, prefabricated homes, hair curlers, and helicopters should not be sold on the same basis." J. Gordon Lippincott, *Design for Business,* 1947.

ABOVE *Marshall McLuhan's 1951 essay "The Mechanical Bride" dissects an ad for stockings. For McLuhan, the disembodied legs in the ad are as standardized as the parts of a machine.*

Until recently, the ideal of the white, middle-class family promoted by most advertising consisted of stay-at-home mothers and employed fathers. Despite this mythic image, however, economic necessity and personal ambition have brought women steadily into the work force over the past two centuries. In the late 1800s, keyboards, switchboards, and telephones became central to new urban, female-identified jobs. This movement of women into employment has been marked by the conflict between their domestic obligations and desires, and their opportunities and expectations as wage-earners.[3] Some employers and unions have capitalized on this conflict by invoking the ideal of domesticity to discourage women from competing with men for wages and to characterize their work as temporary and nonessential. The domestic ideal also has functioned to define women as naturally suited to jobs involving neatness, courtesy, and personal service.

Accompanying women's dramatic entry into the work force in the 1950s and 1960s was a growing awareness among women of how the home shapes female identity. Betty Friedan fueled the postwar revival of feminism with the publication of her 1963 book *The Feminine Mystique.*[4] Friedan studied the media culture of housework, locating in domestic advertisements and magazine features a powerful ideology that limits the ambitions of middle-class housewives. Friedan's book draws on the personal archives of consumer researcher Ernst Dichter, who used emotional appeals to sell appliances and other goods to women.

Friedan's feminist critique of consumer culture was part of a broader critical look at the aesthetic and psychological power of commercial media. Marshall McLuhan's 1951 book *The Mechanical Bride: Folklore of Industrial Man* includes an essay about depictions of the female body as a machine-like aggregate of detachable, interchangeable parts, a pattern McLuhan found in the croppings and juxtapositions of photographs in journalism and advertising. His phrase *mechanical bride* recalls the Dada and Surrealist fascination with sex and technology. Marcel Duchamp, Man Ray, and other avant-garde artists had seen eroticism and destruction—not just rationality—in machines; McLuhan recognized a similar impulse in everyday media.[5]

"Marriage today is not only the culmination of a romantic attachment... it is also a decision to create a partnership in establishing a comfortable home, equipped with a great number of desirable products...."

Ernst Dichter, quoted in Betty Friedan, *The Feminine Mystique,* 1963.

By looking seriously at popular media, Betty Friedan and Marshall McLuhan studied their own society in the way anthropologists examine foreign cultures. They set precedents for the field now called cultural studies, which examines the relationship between artifacts—from consumer goods to city plans—and their social context.[6] While history traditionally focuses on written documents, and art history values rare and precious objects, cultural studies turns to the material remnants of everyday life. For cultural studies, objects do not have a stable meaning, decreed by their makers and frozen in their formal structure (materials, style, technique). Instead, meaning emerges through social practices, including an object's representation in various media, its connection to shared customs, and its significance to the people who own or operate it.

ABOVE *The Dirt Devil vacuum cleaner is a contemporary "fetish." The machine's subtly anthropomorphic shape and distinctive red hue, as well as its explicitly figurative name and logo, animate the machine with a "personality," adding value beyond its utilitarian function.*

Advertising and design serve to amplify the value of useful things, transforming functional tools into appealing commodities that promise to satisfy emotional as well as material needs. The Eureka vacuum cleaner advertised ABOVE RIGHT claims not only to sweep the rug, but to give its user all her "heart desires." Scholars of religion traditionally have used the word *fetish* to describe objects that societies invest with the magical ability to control the forces of nature. The witch's broom, a fetish from European folklore, is a cleaning tool employed for magical purposes; the witch is a dangerously bad housekeeper, a single woman with cobwebs in every corner. Karl Marx borrowed the word *fetish* to characterize the cult object of capitalism: the commodity.[7] In a consumer economy, objects are manufactured primarily to be sold, and only secondarily to satisfy a human need. The object becomes a fetish as its functional aspects give way to psychological incentives. The inanimate object *speaks* through advertising, packaging, styling, and brand name recognition. The corporate personality invoked by a familiar brand name such as the Hoover Company's logo can raise the value of an appliance, regardless of its functional difference from other brands.

> "Since buying is only the climax of a complicated relationship, based to a large extent on the woman's yearning to know how to be a more attractive woman, a better housewife, a superior mother, etc., use this motivation in all your promotion and advertising...."
>
> Ernst Dichter, quoted in Betty Friedan, *The Feminine Mystique,* 1963.

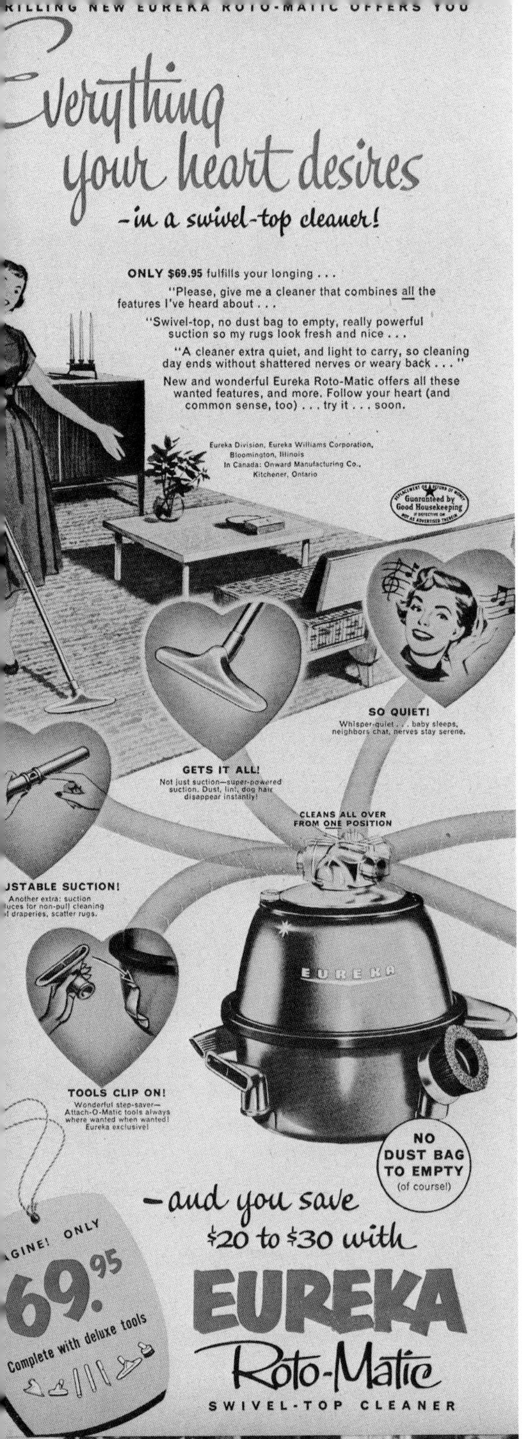

KILLING NEW EUREKA ROTO-MATIC OFFERS YOU

Everything your heart desires -in a swivel-top cleaner!

ONLY $69.95 fulfills your longing . . .

"Please, give me a cleaner that combines all the features I've heard about . . .

"Swivel-top, no dust bag to empty, really powerful suction so my rugs look fresh and nice . . .

"A cleaner extra quiet, and light to carry, so cleaning day ends without shattered nerves or weary back . . ."

New and wonderful Eureka Roto-Matic offers all these wanted features, and more. Follow your heart (and common sense, too) . . . try it . . . soon.

Eureka Division, Eureka Williams Corporation, Bloomington, Illinois
In Canada: Onward Manufacturing Co., Kitchener, Ontario

Guaranteed by Good Housekeeping

SO QUIET! Whisper-quiet . . . baby sleeps, neighbors chat, nerves stay serene.

GETS IT ALL! Not just suction—super-powered suction. Dust, lint, dog hair disappear instantly!

CLEANS ALL OVER FROM ONE POSITION

JSTABLE SUCTION! Another extra: suction luces for non-pull cleaning of draperies, scatter rugs.

EUREKA

TOOLS CLIP ON! Wonderful step-saver—Attach-O-Matic tools always where wanted when wanted! Eureka exclusive!

NO DUST BAG TO EMPTY (of course)

GINE! ONLY 69.95 Complete with deluxe tools

-and you save $20 to $30 with EUREKA Roto-Matic SWIVEL-TOP CLEANER

"I only had one dream where she [my mother] was naked.... She was vacuuming. It wasn't sexual. It was about cleanliness." Nicolas Cage in *Honeymoon in Vegas*, 1992.

Marx assigned a feminine personality to the commodity fetish by describing the alluring, extra-functional features of the consumer product as "amorous glances" that solicit the inner hopes and passions of the buyer. Freud used the word *fetish* to name an inanimate thing or an isolated body part that becomes a substitute for a forbidden sexual object. A foot or a shoe, a hand or a handbag—each can become the target of desire, invested with intense emotional significance.[8]

The fetish, whether sexual, economic, or both, is an object that acquires magical functions. Advertising and design have compared machines to living things by picturing them as extensions, substitutes, metaphors, or erotic mates for the human body. Women, in their roles as consumers and workers, have been wed to technology; meanwhile, the design and promotion of machines have borrowed physical and emotional attributes from women, making domestic appliances and office equipment into glamorous but hard-working brides themselves.

Technology also is fetishized when it is viewed as an independent, autonomously developing organism, capable of altering society by itself and evolving into steadily improving forms. All technologies, from the washing machine to the atom bomb, are invented and used by human beings; they often are used by one group at the expense of another. The myth of an inexorable technological progress fuels the notion that household appliances have consistently liberated women. To study design from a feminist perspective, one must look at the social framework in which objects are put to work.

LEFT *In the 1983 film* Mr. Mom, *unemployed dad Michael Keaton keeps house while his wife goes to work as an ad executive. Keaton battles with hostile appliances—including a runaway vacuum cleaner possessed with a will of its own—before becoming the perfect househusband. The film ends up affirming the domestic norm; rather than share housework, the couple neatly reverses roles.*

"What is domesticated woman?... She only becomes a domestic, a wife, a chattel, a playboy bunny, a prostitute, or a human dictaphone in certain [social] relationships. Torn from those relationships, she is no more the helpmate of man than gold itself is money...."

Gayle Rubin, "The Traffic in Women," 1975.

A person articulates herself *as female* in part through the material objects and images that frame her daily activities. "Gender" is the set of behavioral norms and expectations that members of a given society attribute to the physical differences between women and men. In the words of anthropologist Gayle Rubin, who has analysed the difference between biological "sex" and cultural "gender," the making of a woman is a social process.[9] Feminist studies of design and technology look at products, buildings, cities, and media in relation to women users. Although the built environment is designed largely by men, much of it is constructed with female consumers in mind; design thus contributes to the "making" of modern women.[10]

The following pages offer brief biographies of key objects from the history of industrial design, including the washing machine, telephone, and typewriter—objects that are central to the representation and practice of "women's work." The voices of these inanimate things can be found in media images that suggest how they have been marketed, used, and imagined.

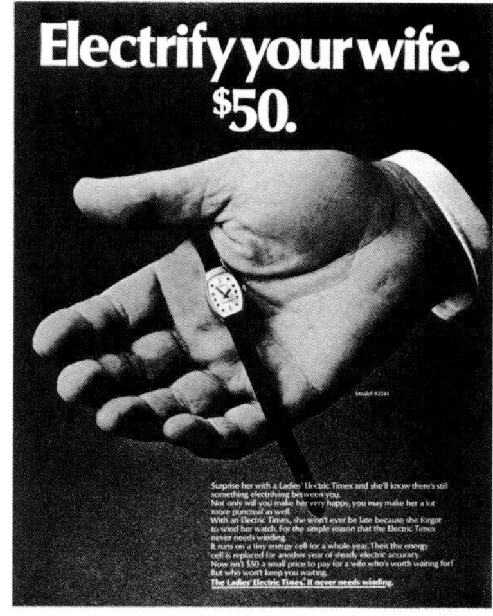

ABOVE *The RCA ad, 1966, compares a television set to a woman—both have lovely faces and sturdy, dependable backsides; courtesy General Electric. The Timex ad, 1969, invites husbands to electrify their wives with a $50 watch.*

LEFT *Drawing on the convention of anthropomorphic consumer products, Laurene Leon designed prototypes in 1992 for a family of kitchen appliances based on characters from the* Wizard of Oz. *Shown here are the Tin Man coffee maker, the Scarecrow crockpot, and the Cowardly Lion tea cozy.*

ABOVE A woman embraces her silicone-covered ironing board. Magla Products, 1956.
LEFT A young couple looks out from a TV set at a landscape of appliances. General American Transportation Corporation, 1957.

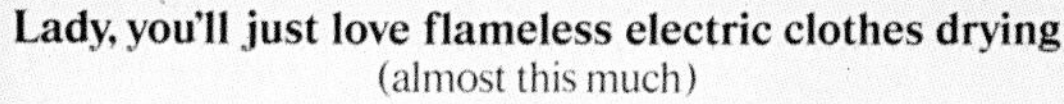

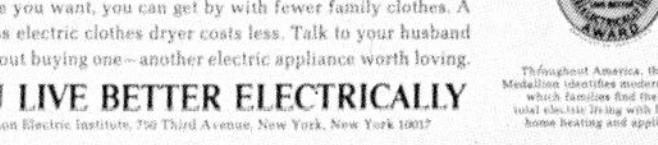

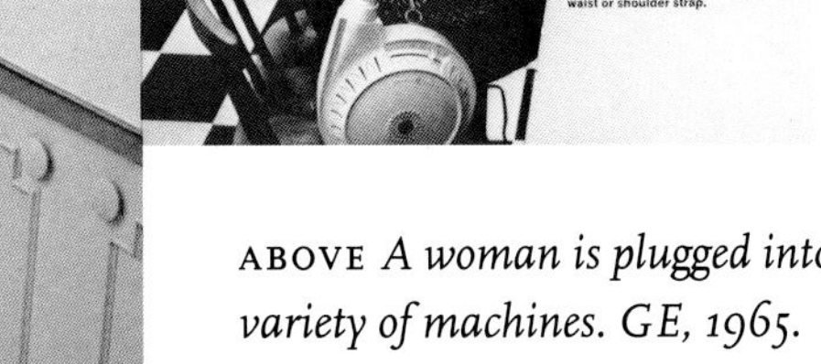

ABOVE A woman is plugged into a variety of machines. GE, 1965.

LEFT A family gathers around Mom as she emblazons her new washing machine with a heart. Edison Electric Institute, 1966.

Keep all kinds of food *market-fresh*—with fewer trips to the market. Five kinds of cold are needed *and provided* in this roomy Westinghouse Refrigerator.

Clean rugs wear longer; another reason for this deep-cleaning, sensibly priced Vacuum Cleaner.

Two happy routes to carefree cooking—the Westinghouse Electric Range and the Roaster-Oven. Both cook tempting meals without watching or worrying. Either assures more free time!

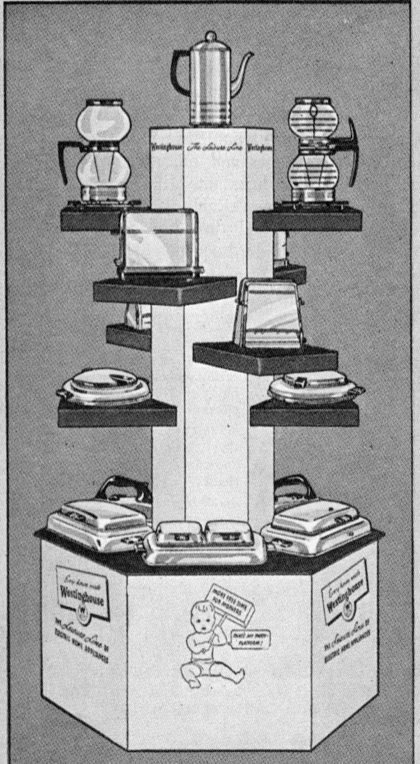

Get an eyeful of this display of electrical smartness—at your near-by Westinghouse dealer's store.

Here's a home laundry that can give "one-day service"—with no wear or tear on your disposition, no strain on your purse—the Westinghouse Washer, Ironer and Streamline Iron.

Every house needs
Westinghouse

W WESTINGHOUSE ELECTRIC

THE *Leisure Line* OF
ELECTRIC HOME APPLIANCES

Tune in "Musical Americana," N.B.C. Red Network, Coast-to-Coast, every Thursday evening.

LOVE, LEISURE, AND *Laundry*

While for men, the ideal American home is a haven from work, for women it is defined as a site for labor. The spread of mechanical appliances, which were promoted as freeing women from their chores, coincided with rising standards of domestic duty.

Feminist historians of technology and design have revised the fairy-tale narrative in which household appliances rescue American women from domestic drudgery.[1] Although modern dwellings have been populated with a myriad of sleek mechanical appliances, standards of cleanliness and child care rose dramatically between 1920 and 1960, leaving women with *more* work rather than less. In the domestic economy of "labor-saving" devices, work saved on one task often diverts to another. Furthermore, the tasks performed with kitchen and laundry equipment have remained associated with women. By glamorizing appliances as partners in achieving health and happiness, advertising and design have encouraged women to embrace housework as women's "natural" calling.

ABOVE LEFT *The woman reclining in this photo from an article on home decorating is not simply resting; she is also babysitting. The washing machine and scrub bucket in the foreground suggest chores in progress.* American Home, *1958.*

ABOVE RIGHT *In contrast, the man who has "Come home to Barcalounger" is at the end of his day of paid labor; he occupies a private, masculine space. 1973.*

FACING PAGE *In this 1940 ad for Westinghouse's "Leisure Line" of domestic appliances, the celebratory message of "more free time for mothers" is undercut by guilt and obligation—the baby explains that new appliances will help his mother meet rising standards of domestic hygiene.*

Laundry is one of the heaviest burdens for housekeepers without access to plumbing and power. Automatic laundry equipment was used in commercial establishments in the nineteenth century, and was transferred to the home in the motorized domestic appliances of the 1920s. Rather than sell a few large machines to centralized businesses, manufacturers sought to sell many smaller units to private households. The return of laundry to the home affirmed women's roles as consumers of individual products instead of shared central services.

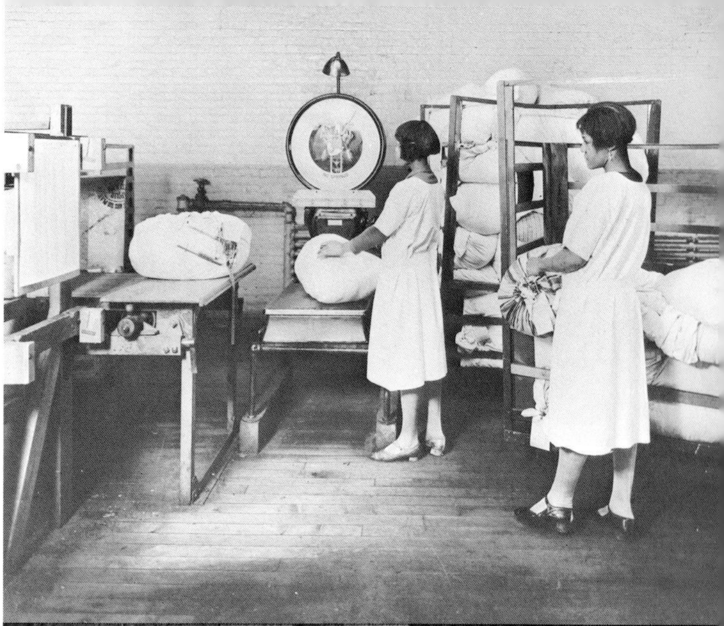

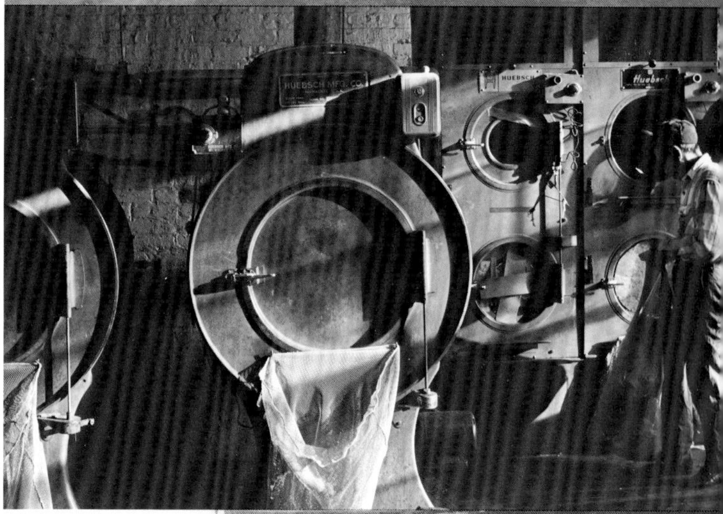

Industrialization took many production activities out of the hands of families in the nineteenth century, from the growing and preserving of food to the manufacture of textiles and clothing. Commercial laundries were founded in the 1830s to serve bachelors in gold mining towns and seaports. Some of the technical innovations that later would be applied to domestic washing machines were first developed for commercial laundries. Employed initially for the care of men's shirts, suits, and collars, centralized steam laundries increasingly were used for "family washes" after the 1890s, a practice that grew steadily through the 1920s, when the commercial laundry business reached its height. Various services were available, from complete washing and ironing to deliveries of damp articles to be "finished" at home. By 1900 families from nearly all economic groups in urban areas had some portion of their laundry done by industrial services or by hired washerwomen.[2]

The use of commercial laundry services was a contested issue at the turn of the century. Although some domestic writers warned against contamination from other people's laundry, members of the progressive home economics movement, founded in the 1890s, tended to favor the practice of removing laundry work from the home and placing it in professionally operated facilities with regulated prices, wages, and working conditions.[3] Playing on racism and xenophobia, large commercial establishments promoted their technologically advanced services as superior to the unschooled labors of the "ignorant washer-woman" (commonly black) or the suspect practices of the "hand laundry" (often run by Chinese-American families).[4]

The marketing of effective home washing machines in the 1920s posed a serious challenge to the flourishing laundry business. Coin-operated "laundromats," opening in the late 1930s, served as a transition between the commercial laundry and the home washing machine by teaching women to use equipment that would be affordable to middle-class families after World War II.

TOP LEFT *Commercial laundries were a major source of employment for African-American women during the 1920s, when the industry was at its peak. Photo, 1928, Museum of the City of New York, Byron Collection.*

MIDDLE LEFT *Beginning in the 1880s, Chinese-Americans operated "hand laundries," which competed with larger steam establishments. Laundry remains an important business for Chinese and other Asians living in American cities. Photo, "Wet Wash," by Paul Calhoun, 1981. Chinatown History Museum, New York.*

BOTTOM LEFT *This ad for the Hoover Company, which ran in* Ebony *in 1967, promotes the individually owned washing machine as the most dignified vehicle for doing the family's wash.*

TOP RIGHT *The postwar "cleaning woman," who works for several families on a live-out basis, carried forward the precedent of the laundress working for hire. Photo, 1977, Library of Congress, U.S. News & World Report Collection.*

The commercial laundry business, damaged by the Depression, regained strength briefly after World War II and then weakened in the 1950s, when appliance ownership became the standard to which most Americans aspired. Historian Ruth Schwartz Cowan attributes the retreat of laundry back into the home to America's commitment to private property and private family life; economist Juliet B. Schor credits it to the low value placed on women's leisure—since the economic worth of a housewife's time typically is unacknowledged, owning home machines is judged as a savings.[5]

In addition to commercial laundries, women working for hire offered an alternative at the turn of the century to families doing their own wash. In the southern states, laundresses (mostly African-American) were employed by all but the poorest urban white families, and by many black families as well.[6] Although laundry was exhausting, numerous women preferred it to working as live-in maids because it enabled them to set their own hours and maintain their own homes and families. With the black migration to the North through the 1930s, the practice of "live-out," part-time domestic service broadened. Although the demand for laundresses fell with the rise of both commercial laundries and mechanical washers, the laundress was the prototype for the postwar "cleaning woman," a domestic worker employed by several families. Because housework has low social and economic value, it continues to be relegated to women and minorities. Whether performed by an unpaid housewife or by a cleaning woman working without benefits, housework is an invisible, underground economy.

"I worked for a woman, her husband's a judge. I cleaned the whole house. When it was time for me to go home, she decided she wants some ironing. She goes in the basement, she turns on the air conditioner. She said, 'I think you can go down in the basement and finish your day out. It's air conditioned.' I said, 'I don't care what you got down there, I'm not ironing. You look at that slip, it says cleanin'. Don't say no ironin'."

Maggie Holmes, former domestic worker, interviewed by Studs Terkel in *Working*, 1975.

LEFT *This 1941 GE ad monumentalizes an appliance that many women have viewed with ambivalence.*

BELOW *Lily Tomlin is engulfed by a larger-than-life kitchen in* The Incredible Shrinking Woman, *1980.*

Sociologists have studied the influence of domestic technology on women's time use. Looking at a 1965–66 national survey of urban households, Joann Vanek found that work force participation, *not* possession of appliances, affected the time spent on housework—employed wives devoted an average of twenty-six hours per week to their domestic duties, as compared to fifty-five hours by nonemployed women. Vanek found that the hours nonemployed wives spent on cleaning, cooking, shopping, and childcare rose from 52 hours a week in the 1920s to 55 in the mid 1960s.[7] While media reports since the "sexual revolution" of the 1970s imply that women no longer do most of the housework, the data suggest otherwise. A 1978 study concluded that although employed women were spending less time on housework than full-time homemakers, they were still doing the same *proportion* relative to men.[8] Reports that housekeeping standards have declined since the mid 1980s blame the lack of time in fully employed households.[9] Arlie Hochschild closely observed a group of double-income families across the period from 1980 to 1988; she found that employed women still were doing most of the housework, a burden assumed during the "second shift" following the day of paid labor. Added to the wage gap between women and men in the work place is the "leisure gap" at home.[10]

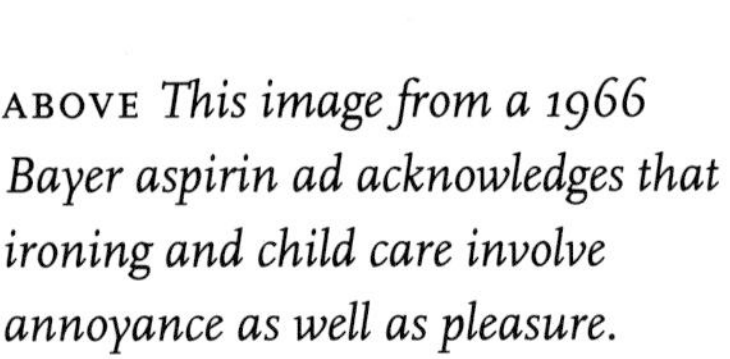

ABOVE *This image from a 1966 Bayer aspirin ad acknowledges that ironing and child care involve annoyance as well as pleasure.*

"For a hundred dollars down we could move into a house [in Levittown] that had venetian blinds, a washing machine, a refrigerator....The house was surrounded by a lake of mud. But I was thrilled—it was a very exciting thing to have a house of your own. You got a beautiful stainless steel sink with two drains, cabinets, drawers, a three-burner General Electric stove with oven, a Bendix washing machine. The only thing I had to buy...was a fluorescent tube over the kitchen sink—the fixture was even there."

Cele Roberts, interviewed about her 1949 move to Levittown by Brett Harvey in *The Fifties: A Women's Oral History*, 1993.

Advertisers promised women new leisure time by endowing appliances with the magical power to do "all the work" of housekeeping—the machine poses as an electric servant or a substitute self with a mechanical body and brain. Ad campaigns for Bendix in the 1940s promoted the machine's ability to free women for leisure activities, such as shopping, entertaining, or relaxing. Bendix washing machines were installed as part of the purchase price of homes in Levittown and other postwar suburban developments, which are located away from centralized services.

While automatic laundry equipment simplified one of the most arduous tasks of housekeeping, it by no means eliminated human effort altogether. Some *person* still has to gather and sort, load and unload, iron and fold the wash. Furthermore, what appears at first glance to be female leisure is often another form of caregiving, from tending children to serving breakfast.

ABOVE LEFT AND RIGHT *Ads for Bendix automatic washers, 1946 and 1947, celebrate the leisure made possible by new technology. Courtesy of Allied Signal, formerly the Bendix Corporation.*

LEFT *"Mexican woman washing clothes." Photo by Russell Lee, 1939, San Antonio, Texas. FSA, Library of Congress.*

For poor women, especially in rural areas, pre-industrial methods of doing laundry prevailed into the twentieth century. In households without plumbing, buckets of water were hauled from a well; the laundry was then soaked, scrubbed, rinsed, and wrung out by hand before being hung to dry. Laundry traditionally was a two-day process, with Monday reserved for washing and Tuesday for ironing. The woman ABOVE has set her tub on a chair, bringing it within her reach and thus designing a better tool out of existing domestic objects. Households today without access to automatic laundry equipment utilize whatever facilities they do have, from the kitchen sink to the bathtub. The cleaning action employed in hand washing is *friction*: wet fabric is rubbed against itself or against a ribbed washboard. Many of the nearly two thousand U.S. patents for washing machines filed during the nineteenth century imitate the rubbing action of hand laundry with mechanical "dollies" that pound the fabric.[11]

Modern washing machines employ *agitation* rather than friction; they circulate soapy water through the fabric, which carries away dirt and results in less wear on the garments. The electrically powered home washers introduced in the 1910s consisted of tubs equipped with a revolving agitator; to keep the clothes from tangling, the agitator reversed direction—a principle employed in commercial laundries since the mid-nineteenth century. When the cycle was complete, the user passed each garment through the wringer, watching for easily broken buttons. Washers not permanently plumbed had to be filled and drained by hand. Early models resembled motorized washtubs standing on legs; designers after the mid 1930s began rationalizing the machine, hiding the motor behind a metal skirt (Thor, 1936, ABOVE LEFT) or integrating the legs with the enameled body and encasing the wringer in a smooth shell (Speed Queen, 1948, ABOVE RIGHT).

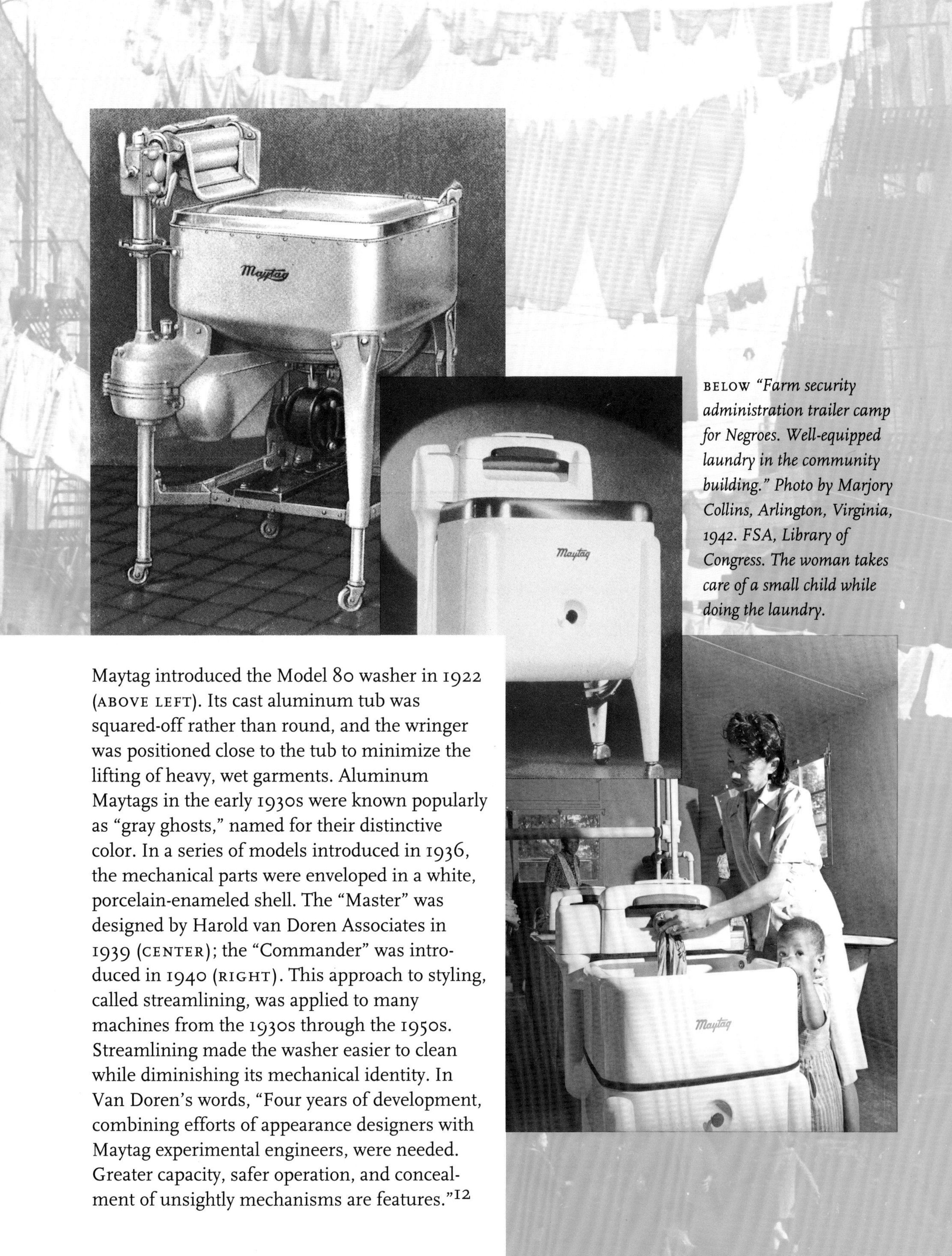

BELOW *"Farm security administration trailer camp for Negroes. Well-equipped laundry in the community building." Photo by Marjory Collins, Arlington, Virginia, 1942. FSA, Library of Congress. The woman takes care of a small child while doing the laundry.*

Maytag introduced the Model 80 washer in 1922 (ABOVE LEFT). Its cast aluminum tub was squared-off rather than round, and the wringer was positioned close to the tub to minimize the lifting of heavy, wet garments. Aluminum Maytags in the early 1930s were known popularly as "gray ghosts," named for their distinctive color. In a series of models introduced in 1936, the mechanical parts were enveloped in a white, porcelain-enameled shell. The "Master" was designed by Harold van Doren Associates in 1939 (CENTER); the "Commander" was introduced in 1940 (RIGHT). This approach to styling, called streamlining, was applied to many machines from the 1930s through the 1950s. Streamlining made the washer easier to clean while diminishing its mechanical identity. In Van Doren's words, "Four years of development, combining efforts of appearance designers with Maytag experimental engineers, were needed. Greater capacity, safer operation, and concealment of unsightly mechanisms are features."[12]

BELOW *A Bendix automatic washer rises above a landscape of obsolete wringer-type machines in this illustration from an ad in* Fortune, *1947. Glittering on the hand that holds the machine is a diamond engagement ring.*

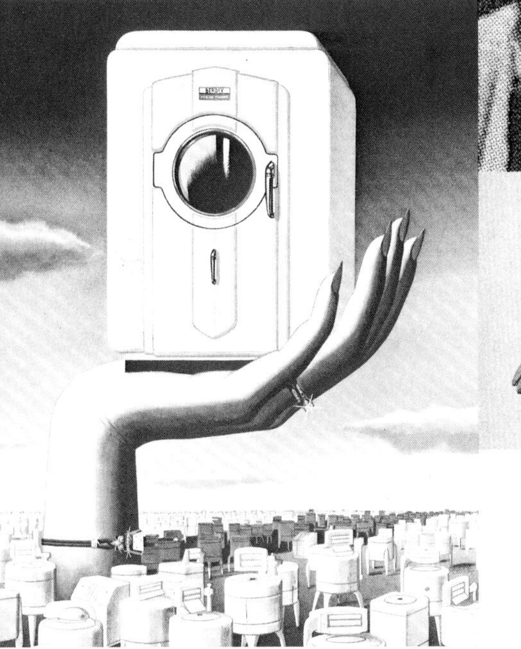

The Bendix automatic washing machine ABOVE was available as early as 1938, and was widely promoted in the late 1940s. The machine fills and drains automatically; it is equipped with a perforated inner drum that "spins dry" the fabric between cycles. While the cubic box around the cylindrical drum conceals the mechanical aspects of the appliance, the glass window reveals the machine's tumbling action, enabling the user to watch it work.[13]

The Duomatic was another Bendix innovation. As advertised ABOVE in *Ebony* in 1954, the Duomatic is a combined automatic washer and dryer. Like other front-loading washers, the machine has no central agitator, but works by the "tumble action" of a revolving inner cylinder. The same action is used to dry the garments after the tub has been emptied. A 1953 trade article heralded the two-in-one concept of the Duomatic as "the key to future product-design thinking for small homes."[14] Despite its efficient use of space and materials, however, the combined washer-dryer failed to become a household norm.

While most automatic washers load from either the top or the side, Westinghouse's "Laundromat," advertised ABOVE in 1948, has a slanted front, merging the two dominant types.

ABOVE *The principle of agitation is explained in this 1950 diagram. This agitator moves up and down as well as back and forth, providing "live water action." The Frigidaire Company.*

BELOW LEFT *GE Filter-Flo washer, advertised in 1961.*

By the end of the 1950s, the top-loading automatic washing machine, consisting of a cylindrical drum enclosed in a refrigerator-style box, had become the most common type, as it remains today. The form of the typical postwar washer continues the language of the modern kitchen, with its continuous banks of modular work surfaces, appliances, and cabinets. Although numerous home decorating articles from the 1930s onward have advocated separate laundry rooms, many of them acknowledge that households tend to tuck washing machines into multi-use spaces, such as basements, kitchens, bathrooms, utility rooms, or hallways.[15]

ABOVE *Dashboards of square buttons replaced round knobs in the 1950s and early 1960s. Design historian Thomas Hine has described the period as the age of the push button in appliance design. Maytag, 1960.*

The chief design variations among machines from the 1950s and 1960s are found in color, control panels, and special features such as softener dispensers and inner baskets for delicates. The hallmark colors of the 1950s were pink, turquoise, and sunshine yellow, the late 1960s heralded the "organic" palette of copper, avocado, and harvest gold. Advertised ABOVE RIGHT is the Whirlpool Corporation's 1969 avocado dryer with wood-grained paneling, whose timer turns the dryer back on when the machine is not attended. The decorator hues of the 1950s and 1960s accelerated product obsolescence by encouraging families to redesign their kitchens around new appliances. Today, the most popular washer colors are neutral white and almond. Key design concerns since the 1970s have included energy- and water-efficiency and reduced sizes for apartments and for small households. Stacked washer-and-dryer "twins" were marketed as early as 1958, but only recently have become a popular type.[16]

The use of heat and pressure to flatten fabric dates back at least to the Renaissance. The nineteenth-century “sad iron,” consisting of a prow-shaped soleplate with a handle attached, was designed to be heated on a coal or wood stove. Mary Florence Potts improved on the sad iron in 1871 by designing a detachable wooden handle. The “Mrs. Potts’ iron,” BELOW LEFT, enabled its user to heat several soleplates simultaneously, while the handle remains cool. Although an electric iron was patented in 1882, it was not a viable home appliance before 1904. Early electric irons such as the 1924 Sunbeam BELOW RIGHT are closely linked to the traditional sad iron. The red iron ABOVE, from the 1930s, replaces the heaviness of solid metal with the heaviness of solid glass.[17]

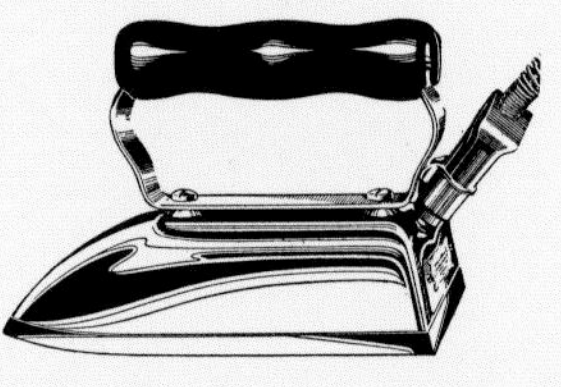

The price of the traditional sad iron depended on its weight—i.e., the amount of material it was physically made of. In the 1930s, manufacturers began to employ styling to distinguish competing irons from one another; qualities such as visual appeal, comfort to the hand, and placement of controls joined technical features such as steam and adjustable thermostats in enhancing the value of irons. The replacement of lathe-turned wooden handles with cast phenolic resin (known by the trade name Bakelite) spawned exuberant design variations. The curved, streamlined styling of the iron TOP LEFT has a primarily decorative function, while the handles of the two irons ABOVE RIGHT attempt to conform to the user’s grasp. The Steam-O-Matic, BOTTOM RIGHT, manufactured in the late 1930s, employs aluminum for its lightness, signalling the shift toward irons that rely on steam rather than weight. The Steam-O-Matic’s design attempts to meld the plastic handle with the metal body, the curves of one flowing into the other.

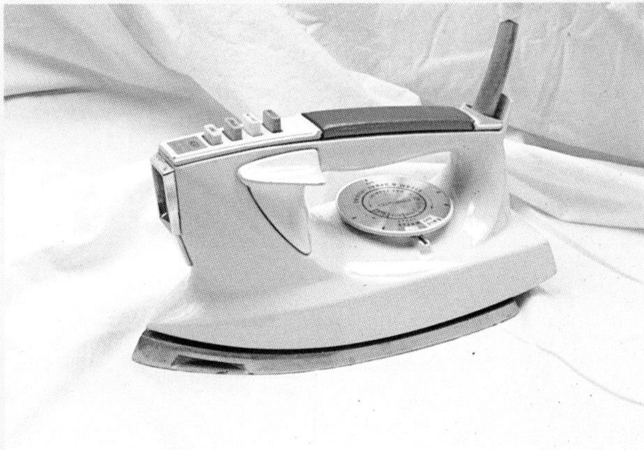

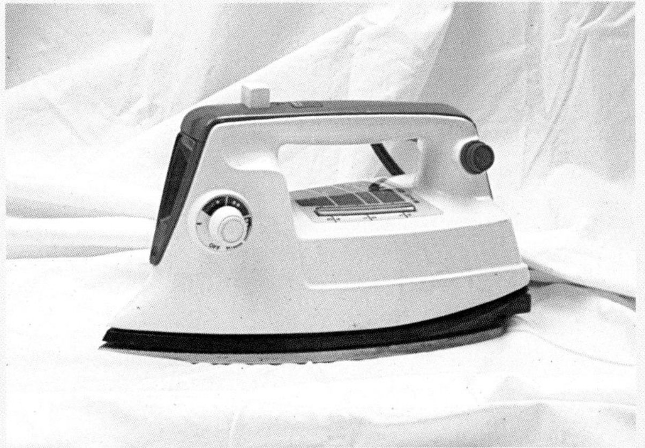

FACING PAGE
(clockwise from upper left)

White Cross, c. 1936
Courtesy Carole Krohn

Open handled iron, 1930s
Courtesy Kate Loye

Steam-O-Matic, c. 1939
Courtesy Marjorie Chester

Glass iron, 1940s
Courtesy Alex Shear/The Nostalgia Brokers, New York

THIS PAGE
(clockwise from upper left)

Casco iron, c. 1957
Courtesy Kate Loye

Presto, 1960
Courtesy Vincent Cracchiolo

Proctor-Silex Lady Light, 1981
Courtesy Vincent Cracchiolo

Mrs. American, model introduced in 1960. Courtesy Marshall Johnson

The handle took on increasing importance in the irons of the 1950s; as a dramatic stage for various controls and identifying graphics, the handle became almost equal in volume to the "skirt" or "shroud." Black phenolic resin has been finished in red in the Casco iron BOTTOM LEFT. The 1960 Presto, TOP RIGHT, is made of phenolic resin painted pale green; the handle has expanded to become the entire skirt of the iron. The Presto is also remarkable for its ambidexterous controls and a cord that juts straight out of the back, rather than favoring the right side. Proctor-Silex's 1981 Lady Light, BOTTOM RIGHT, was the first American iron with a skirt made of thermoset plastic, a heat-resistant material that is colored all the way through.[18] Cordless irons were marketed as early as 1948, but continue today to be a frustrating product, as the iron must constantly be returned to its base for reheating—like the nineteenth-century sad iron, which had to be repeatedly returned to the stove.

ABOVE *Special cycles accommodate a variety of new fabrics, Hotpoint, 1960. Courtesy General Electric.*

Washing machines and irons operate in the context of numerous other products, from detergents and bleaches to fabric and fashion. Not only were domestic washing machines transformed in the decades around World War II, but laundry itself was reconceived. The rising popularity of "wash and wear" synthetics and new fabric finishes in the 1950s minimized some domestic ironing chores. At the same time, the new materials encouraged the home laundering of articles that might previously have been sent out, including men's shirts, pants, and even suits.[19] Washing machine manufacturers responded to the new materials by designing machines with variable settings, including a warm wash/cold rinse cycle that reduces the wrinkling of permanent press fabric.

ABOVE *Ad for a Dacron wash and wear suit, DuPont, 1958.*

BELOW *Advertising photo promoting Sanforized fabric, 1960. The Sanforized Company, a division of Cluett, Peabody & Co., Inc.*
CENTER *Three-ring agitator, Frigidaire, 1958.*

"Feminists need to take a serious, sustained, and sympathetic interest in the home....The sharing of housework is unlikely to occur if women continue the denigration of its value—why would men want to help if the work is seen as degrading, humiliating, and economically worthless?... If [housework] is despised, it will be performed by someone whose sex, class, or race—perhaps all three—consign her to an inferior status."
Glenna Matthews, *Just a Housewife*, 1987.

The care of manufactured goods is one of the central labors of the industrialized household. Historian Michael Thompson has used the phrase *rubbish theory* to name the changing economic value of objects—the gold of one era is the garbage of another.[20] Like economic value, an object's need for cleaning and care changes across its life. In a constant cycle, today's garments become tomorrow's laundry; dinner-at-eight becomes dirty dishes at nine. Recognition of this unavoidable cycle has led some feminists to question Betty Friedan's *Feminine Mystique*. Only after the social and economic importance of keeping house is acknowledged will the home be celebrated as a site of mutual pleasure and responsibility for the sexes.

"The Voice with a Smile"

"Hail ye small, sweet courtesies of life, for smooth do ye make the road of it."

Often we hear comments on the courtesy of telephone people and we are mighty glad to have them.

For our part, we would like to say a word about the courtesy of those who use the telephone.

Your co-operation is always a big help in maintaining good telephone service and we want you to know how much we appreciate it.

BELL TELEPHONE SYSTEM

THE VOICE WITH A *Smile*

What can a telephone communicate? While a typical phone appears to be a neutral channel for information, with no message of its own, telephones have been a link—both symbolic and electric—between the gendered worlds of the home and the office.

ABOVE *Image from a recruitment ad for AT&T in* American Girl, *1943. The copy explains that the ratio of female to male employees at Bell was 3 to 2. Ayer Collection, Smithsonian Institution.*

If judged by appearances alone, the telephone might seem to be the very prototype of a value-free, gender-neutral object. A telephone aspires to be a passive tool rather than an active author; it is a messenger but not a message. The design ambition behind many telephones is, in fact, to *disappear* as an object, becoming a transparent frame for the conversation it hosts.[1] Yet despite the seeming neutrality of the telephone, its use in homes and offices has shaped and reflected gender differences.

ABOVE *Henry Dreyfuss Associates designed telephones and operators' headsets for AT&T beginning in the 1930s. This sketch by Dreyfuss pokes fun at attempts to camouflage the technological identity of the phone.* Designing for People, *1955.*
FACING PAGE *Ad for AT&T, 1949. The operator's headset was designed by Dreyfuss Associates.*

Many jobs pegged as "women's work" in the twentieth century center on the phone, including secretary, receptionist, customer service agent, and telephone operator. In each of these occupations, women regulate the flow of information by taking messages, transferring calls, receiving orders, dialing for the boss, etc. Such jobs make the female worker a human extension of a technological system, charged with mediating—rather than producing—messages.

Cultural expectations about the behavior of female employees parallel expectations about communications devices: both are asked to serve as passive hosts to a drama played out by others. AT&T's slogan "The Voice with a Smile," used from the 1930s through the 1950s, *visualizes* the cheerful sound of the company's female agents and operators, painting a pretty face on the happy voice of the phone worker. This smiling voice is an asset in many modern offices, where the secretary who intercepts calls signifies an executive's status.[2]

LEFT *This 1914 AT&T ad illustration shows the shift from men walking along a wall of switches to seated women making connections within arm's reach. Ayer Collection, Smithsonian Institution.*

“The dulcet tones of the feminine voice seem to exercise a soothing and calming effect upon the masculine mind, subduing irritation and suggesting gentleness of speech and demeanor; thereby avoiding unnecessary friction.”

The American Telephone Journal, 1902,
cited in Lana Rakow, “Women and the Telephone.”

The telephone is not just an object, but an element in a vast system of electrical connections and human services. Female switchboard operators, service representatives, and clerical workers have constituted the majority of office-based phone company employees for over a century. By the early 1880s, the occupation of switchboard operator was almost exclusively female. Women were valued not only because they worked for lower wages but because of their gentle voices, nimble fingers, and mild tempers. From the 1930s through the 1950s, AT&T recruited female employees through magazines such as *American Girl, Senior Prom*, and *True Story*. Ads showing dreamy-eyed young women “in love” with their jobs equate long-distance connections with exotic travel, and customer assistance with having “two thousand friends.”

With the introduction of automated switchboards in the early 1920s, the human qualities expected of telephone operators began to be outweighed by demands for speed and efficiency. The speech of operators traditionally has been regulated through strict codes of appropriate responses, enforced by supervisors listening unannounced on operators’ lines or, increasingly, by electronic monitoring systems that record the duration of calls and the time spent between transactions.[3]

ABOVE AND RIGHT *Men and women are associated with technology in different ways, as demonstrated in this pair of AT&T advertising illustrations. For the female telephone operator, the phone line is a maternal bond allied with the Earth, 1939. For the male engineer/executive, the phone is a dynamic vehicle of progress comparable to the train, plane, and automobile, 1920. Ayer Collection, Smithsonian Institution.*

BELOW RIGHT *A wartime ad for wire situates the female operator between the senders and receivers of messages.*
BELOW LEFT *The cartoon literalizes the notion of the female body as a communications technology.*

Approximately 90 percent of phone operators and 75 percent of service representatives were women in 1993. Unionization, initiated by the Communications Workers of America in 1938, has helped combat the low wages that are typical of female-dominated occupations.[4] Today, operators and service representatives working in unionized companies, including NYNEX and AT&T, earn salaries equal to the average of *all* US workers (male and female combined), whereas the average wage earned by female employees in general in 1993 was only 71 cents to the male dollar. These numbers suggest that while female dominated jobs tend to be low paying, workers and managers can cooperate to achieve fair wages.

"The operator must now be made... a paragon of perfection, a kind of human machine, the exponent of speed and courtesy, a creature spirited enough to move like chain lightning, and with perfect accuracy; docile enough to deny herself the sweet privilege of the last word."

Katherine M. Schmitt, "I was your Old Hello Girl," *Saturday Evening Post*, 12 July, 1930. Schmitt was an operator on the first New York telephone exchange and later became an operator trainer.

With his 1964 motto "the medium is the message," Marshall McLuhan argued that communications technologies are not passive conduits for information but influence the way it is produced and used. McLuhan claimed that the phone had levelled pyramids of power by making high executives accessible. Yet McLuhan acknowledged that men and women have different roles to play in the democratized, telephonic office. The secretary mediates between the boss and the phone, providing him with "a general means of harmony [and] an invitation to happiness."[5] She also shields him from unwanted calls in a *too* democratic information environment.

Countless media images have depicted the phone as a partner to female pleasure, both at home and at work. Through such images and the social practices that they reflect and shape, the phone functions not simply as a neutral communications device but as a gendered symbol, a medium with a message.

“You have to have a nice smiling voice. You can’t be angry or come in like you’ve been out the night before....My phone voice is a lot different from my home voice. I can call the switchboard right now and they wouldn’t know me.”

Frances Swenson, hotel switchboard operator, interviewed by Studs Terkel in *Working*, 1975.

“There are about seven or eight phrases that you use....‘Operator, may I help you?’....‘What number did you want?’.... ‘Would you repeat that again?’.... One man said, ‘I’m lonesome, will you talk to me?’ I said, ‘Gee, I’m sorry, I just can’t.’ But you *can’t*. I’m a communications person but I can’t communicate.”

Heather Lamb, long-distance operator, interviewed by Studs Terkel in *Working*, 1975.

ABOVE LEFT *Before World War II the body behind the “voice with a smile” was typically young, white, and single, as seen in this playfully suggestive magazine cover, 1941. © The Curtis Publishing Company.*

ABOVE RIGHT *Telephone work became more diverse in the 1950s, as women from different ethnic, racial, and age groups entered the field. Telephone operators, New York. Schomburg Center, New York Public Library.*

BELOW *Lily Tomlin’s character Ernestine, from the NBC TV show* Laugh In *(1967–1973) is a telephone operator who rejects the ideal of the “voice with a smile.”*

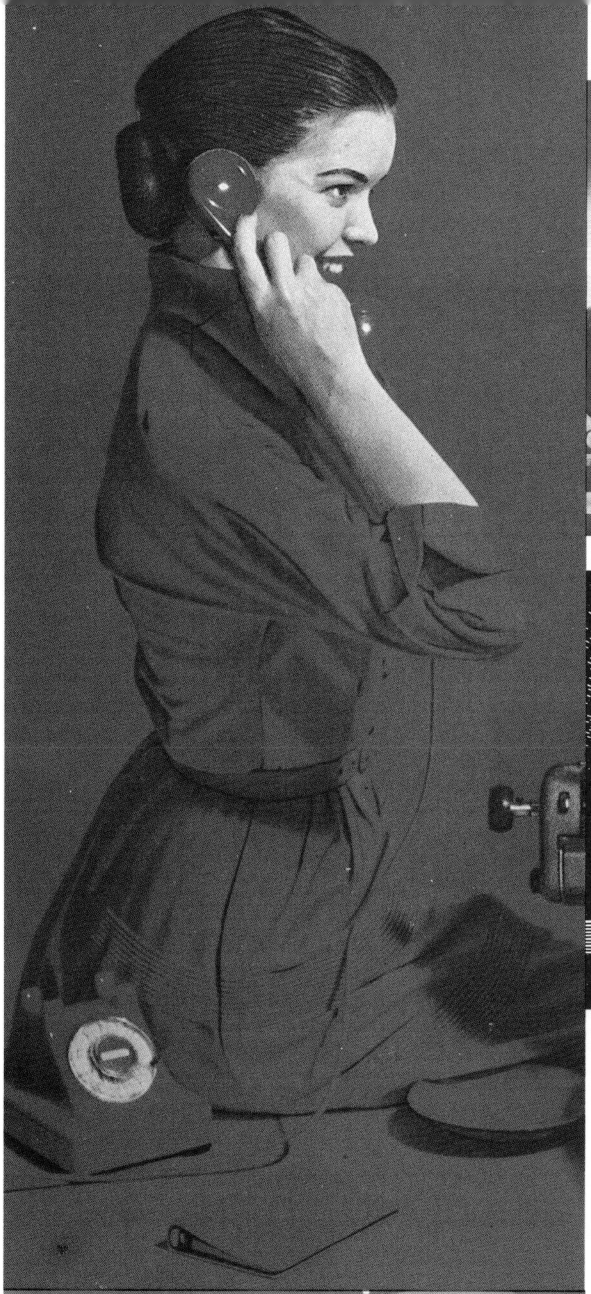

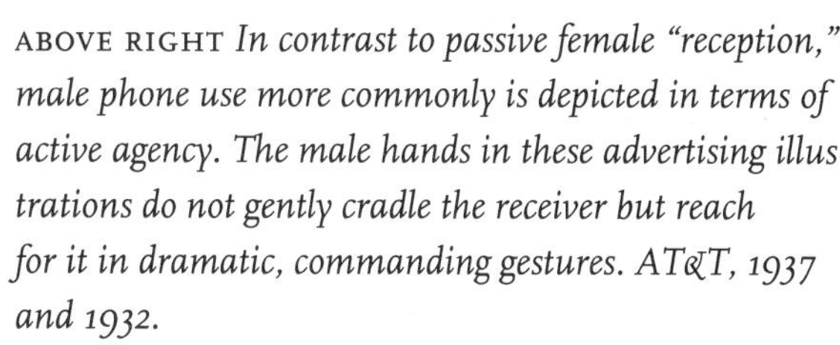

ABOVE RIGHT *In contrast to passive female "reception," male phone use more commonly is depicted in terms of active agency. The male hands in these advertising illustrations do not gently cradle the receiver but reach for it in dramatic, commanding gestures. AT&T, 1937 and 1932.*

TOP LEFT *Colored telephones were promoted primarily to appeal to female consumers and office workers, as seen in this advertising photo for Burroughs accounting equipment, 1953, where a red phone harmonizes with the lipstick-colored world of the secretary.*

BOTTOM LEFT *The red telephone at "Headquarters, Strategic Air Command" has a distinctly masculine association. The copy explains, "Swift, dependable communication is our business, whether to speed the cheerful voices of home and industry or the sterner voices of defense." This Cold War instrument uses red to signify its solemn importance. AT&T, 1959.*

This is one of the most important telephones in the free world

A vital link in the nation's communications network, widely dispersed for safety

The handset, in which the receiver and transmitter are linked by a handle, was patented in England in 1877, just one year after the invention of telephony. Early handsets were problematic, however, because the transmitters were sensitive to movement. While handsets remained common in Europe, the vast distances crossed by U.S. phone lines made efficient transmission a priority. The handset shown in the erotic postcard ABOVE, c. 1900, is assembled out of several different materials. The handle is completely straight, but the cone-shaped mouthpiece reaches toward the speaker.[6]

The "candlestick" was the principal type of telephone used in America between 1892 and the late 1920s. The transmitter is attached to a stationary base, while the receiver is hand held. The height of the candlestick brought the transmitter closer to the user's mouth. The postcard ABOVE, c. 1911, suggests that some phone users preferred to hold the candlestick as well as the earpiece in their hands, negating the design intention behind the fixed base.

Improvements in transmitter design led to the introduction of a handset telephone by Bell in 1927. It was popularly known as the "French" phone, because U.S. veterans had seen similar devices in France during World War I. Made from metal and later plastic, the transmitter curves toward the user's mouth, as seen in the 1932 AT&T advertising photo ABOVE.

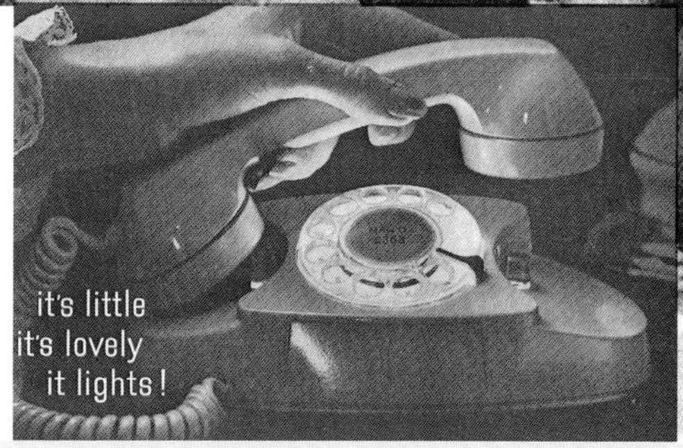

Henry Dreyfuss Associates designed the 300 and 500 Series phones in 1937 and 1949 in collaboration with Bell engineers (ABOVE LEFT and RIGHT). While the older "French" phone has a round base and a narrow neck borrowed from the candlestick, the Dreyfuss designs have low, stocky bodies and rectilinear footprints.

In the 500 phone, the Dreyfuss team maximized the horizontality and continuity of forms; the squared section of the handle prevents it from turning in the user's palm, as seen in the photo TOP, 1966. These rational phones were designed as an extension of AT&T's corporate image rather than as enticing consumer products.[7]

In contrast to the firm's earlier designs for Bell, Dreyfuss Associates' Princess phone appealed directly to female consumers. Released by AT&T in 1959, the Princess was targeted at a primarily female public, including teenagers, who were a recently discovered market (TOP RIGHT). Ads for the new oval-shaped phone emphasize its small size and light-up dial.[8] Petite, horizontal, and cast in decorator colors, the Princess phone suggests a reclining nude. The low profile of the Princess is developed in many subsequent phone designs, including Dreyfuss Associates' own 1965 Trimline and Eric Chan's 1986 Becker EC phone.[9]

The Ericofon at LEFT, designed in 1956 by Ralph Lysell, Hugo Blomberg, and Gosta Thames for the Swedish company Ericsson, was marketed to women by AT&T as an example of high-style modernism. The dial is built into the base of the handset. The verticality of the Ericofon can be seen in the one-piece portables of the 1980s.

BELOW *This postcard celebrates the phone's ability to cross architectural and sexual barriers, c. 1920.*
RIGHT *In another postcard, a man ponders whether to write or phone his lover, c. 1900.*

From the turn of the century through the 1920s, numerous picture postcards place the telephone in romantic scenarios, as seen ABOVE. Through its direct, living access to the ear, the telephone offered a more intimate form of contact than writing a letter. In a society obsessed with feminine virtue, the telephone enabled romantic exchanges between the sexes. Until recently, telephone etiquette discouraged women from initiating phone conversations with men. A 1930 story by Dorothy Parker describes a woman's wait for a phone call from a male acquaintance—in the passage at RIGHT, she blames the inanimate object, not the absent caller, for the phone's excruciating silence.

According to historian Lana Rakow, obscene phone calls did not become a significant problem for women until the nearly universal replacement of shared "party lines" by private lines in the early 1960s. Older phone systems had involved more interaction with operators and neighbors, and thus less anonymity for potential pranksters.

"Look. Suppose a young man says he'll call a girl up, and then something happens, and he doesn't. That isn't so terrible, is it? Why, it's going on all over the world, right this minute.
Oh, what do I care what's going on all over the world? Why can't that telephone ring? Why can't it, why can't it? Couldn't you ring? Ah, please, couldn't you? You damned, ugly, shiny thing.... Damn you, I'll pull your filthy roots out of the wall, I'll smash your smug black face in little bits. Damn you to hell."

Dorothy Parker, "The Telephone Call," 1930.

The intimacy and anonymity facilitated by the telephone has been utilized by the "call girl," a prostitute who makes her contacts over the phone rather than on the streets. In *Understanding Media,* Marshall McLuhan claimed that the telephone had enabled the prostitute to replace her pimp with an answering service and to become an entrepreneur. Nine-hundred-number sex services emerged as a lucrative business in the 1980s, providing the safety of physical distance for buyer and seller alike. Electronic pagers also have become tools for the sex worker. Today, the Bureau of Labor Statistics classifies call girls under the same industry category as other telecommunications workers.

"The first prerequisite [for the call girl] is a telephone in good working order, with an answering service...a clever girl will not phone into the 'office' too frequently when on duty with a fifty- or hundred-dollar man. It is bad taste, as it reminds the buyer that his purchase is not exclusive."

"Stella," interviewed by Harold Greenwald in *The Call Girl,* 1958.

LEFT *In the 1960 film* Butterfield 8, *starring Elizabeth Taylor, the story of a call girl's fall and redemption hinges on the status of her telephone exchange ("Butterfield 8"). The opening shot pans from a powder blue 500 Series phone—off the hook on a nightstand—to Taylor's sleeping body. Throughout the film, Taylor's constant communication with men through her answering service signals her sexual promiscuity. Her attempt to reform herself at the end of the film culminates in her decision to cancel her answering service.*

ABOVE *The maid shown in this 1929 kitchen, from an ad for AT&T, is using a wall-mounted phone, which would be reintroduced as a rotary-dial kitchen phone in 1956.*

While many women were using telephones to earn a living in offices and telephone exchanges by the early twentieth century, at home they were talking on the phone with friends and relatives. Phone companies have not always applauded women's taste for the telephone, as historians Claude S. Fischer and Michèle Martin have documented.[10] Early phone executives had begun their careers in the telegraph industry, whose product was directed primarily at businesses, not consumers. Seeing their technology as a business-to-business service, phone executives dismissed women's talk as "idle chatter" that tied up the lines.

In the 1910s and 1920s, the home phone was promoted primarily as a tool for rational domestic management—that is, for calling the doctor, ordering groceries, or directing the maid, but not for leisurely conversation. In the pair of 1929 ad illustrations at LEFT, a woman and her servant use an internal line to "carry on the household routine efficiently"; the two phones communicate between the traditionally feminine realms of the boudoir and kitchen.

By the late 1920s AT&T marketers realized they should *stimulate* rather than denigrate female phone use. When home subscriptions declined dramatically during the Depression, Bell actively encouraged women to socialize on the phone—women have been the principal targets of domestic phone marketing ever since. Thus marketers came to recognize women's casual phone talk as an economically significant use of a technology that was originally intended for more "serious" purposes. Women have used phones to build personal relationships and to break their isolation in the home; female phone conversation serves nurturing functions while at the same time confirming the belief that these roles "naturally" define women's spheres.

The Telephone Way to a Happier Day

Try it today when the dishes are done, beds made, clothes in the washer. You've earned a break.

So relax a little and pick up the telephone. Enjoy a cheerful visit with a friend or loved one.

It's so easy to do, whatever the miles may be. For no one is ever far away by telephone.

It helps to make any day a happier day at both ends of the line.

"It's fun to phone"

BELL TELEPHONE SYSTEM

ABOVE LEFT AND RIGHT *This pair of AT&T advertising illustrations suggests the difference between men's and women's domestic leisure. The man relaxes without apparent interruption, and his phone is compared to his faithful dog. The woman takes a break from ongoing household chores—a vacuum cleaner lurks behind the woman's armchair. For her, the living room is as much a place of labor as of leisure. AT&T, 1955 and 1958.*

BELOW RIGHT *AT&T's wall phone, designed in 1956, was promoted as the ideal kitchen phone through the 1960s. The instrument takes up no counter space and complements wall-hung cabinets. AT&T, 1965.*

Women's pleasure in talking on the phone at home has been transmitted to the office and switchboard as the "voice with a smile," the cheerful human interface with technology. By weaving together new communication networks, women can find ways to channel the power of conversation to making policy, connecting neighborhoods, and building businesses. Such activities position women to *make* messages as well as *take* messages, and to transfer personal values to the public realm.

FACING PAGE
All photos are details of AT&T ads except for BOTTOM LEFT, *courtesy of Michigan Bell.*

THIS PAGE
Couple talking on blue phone, CENTER, *is from a Pepsi ad, 1965. Woman surrounded by men,* TOP RIGHT, *is from a 1992 ad for The Donna Karan Company.* BOTTOM, *detail of an AT&T ad, 1950.*

THE SHORTEST DISTANCE BETWEEN THE THOUGH

AND THE PERFECTLY TYPEWRITTEN LETTER

IS THE NEW EASY-WRITING ROYAL TYPEWRITE

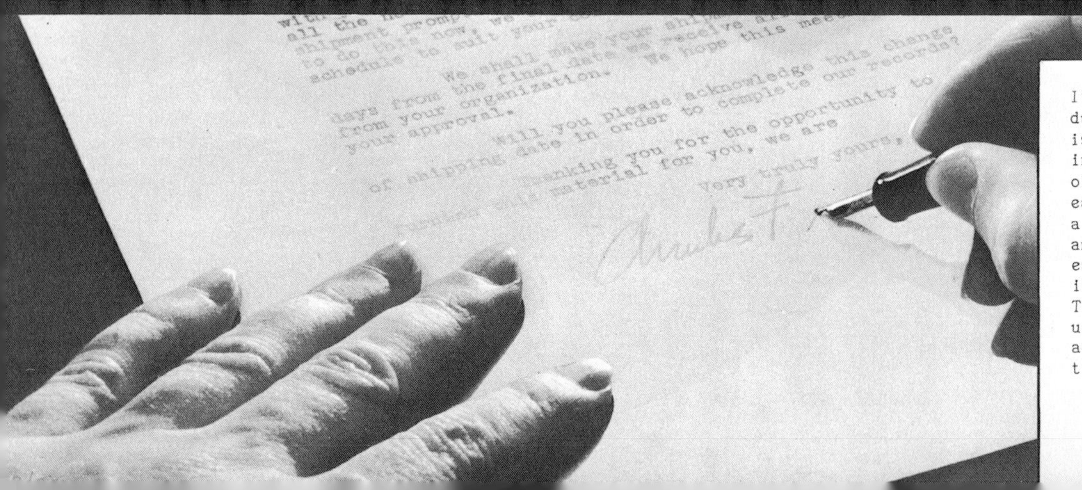

Its acknowledged capacity for reducing the cost of time and effort is verified by spectacular sales increases. Since the introduction of the Victory Model, a year ago, each month has been signalized with a new all-time high record. This amazing acceptance is deserved ... earned by the mechanical superiority of the New Easy-Writing Royal. Touch Control, an exclusive feature, and 17 other major advances, account for its world-wide reputation for finer, faster typing.

ROYAL TYPEWRITER COMPANY, INC.
2 PARK AVENUE, NEW YORK CITY
Branches and Agencies the World Over

OFFICE *Politics*

Most modern clerical occupations, including secretary, typist, stenographer, and keypunch operator, are dominated by women. The design and use of mechanical objects, from telephones and typewriters to furniture engineered for efficiency and comfort, are central to the gendered organization of the modern office.

ABOVE *The turn-of-the-century office gave young women rare access—however circumscribed—to the male world of commerce. Photo from a brochure for Remington typewriters and adding machines. Warshaw Collection, Smithsonian Institution.*

Prior to the 1880s, clerical work was a male occupation involving the writing and filing of letters, invoices, and other documents. A clerk was an entry-level employee who could entertain hopes of upward movement through a firm. As he advanced, a clerk earned a degree of decision-making authority and enjoyed considerable variety and personal autonomy within his daily activities. The term *secretary*, from the same root as *secret*, had carried cultural prestige since the Renaissance, referring to the confidant and deputy of a powerful figure.[1] The feminization of this almost exclusively male world occurred with unprecedented speed at the close of the nineteenth century. By 1890, women held 60 percent of all typing and stenography jobs in the U.S.; by 1900, their share was 77 percent; by 1920, it was 90 percent. Rarely has a field of employment—especially one invested with social status—altered its identity so quickly from male to female.[2]

FACING PAGE *The female worker and her typewriter are positioned between the two moments of male agency: the birth of the idea in the mind of the executive, and the final authorization of his signature. In this information triangle, the woman and her machine act as a technological conduit for male thought. Ad for Royal typewriter, 1935. Courtesy of Royal Consumer Business Products, a division of Olivetti Office USA.*

Several factors contributed to the feminization of office work, including the rising *demand* for clerical employees (owing to the explosion of business communications), and the rising *supply* of educated women (owing to the expansion of public schooling and mass literacy). In a situation that was ripe for the admittance of female employees, the newness of the typewriter served as a wedge into the male domain of the office. Because typewriting was a job with no established sexual history, female typists were not perceived as displacing male clerks. Employers were socially discouraged from hiring women to do men's work, which would mean taking jobs away from fathers and husbands—whose employment was seen as necessary—and giving jobs to lower-paid daughters and wives—whose work was understood as the luxurious pursuit of "pin money." The keyboard, whose very *neutrality* first made it available to women, soon became a defining feature of feminized office work.

TOP *At the turn of the century, the term* typewriter *referred not only to the machine but to the typist herself. "Miss Remington" was a fictional spokesperson for Remington products. Ad, c. 1909.*
BOTTOM *The similarity between the piano and the typewriter was used by manufacturers and employers to suggest that women's agility and musicality make them natural typists. Ad, 1921. Warshaw Collection, Smithsonian Institution.*

Through its newness as an object, the typewriter enabled managers to clear the table for the entrance of a new class of clerical workers with highly circumscribed roles to play. Whereas the traditional clerk often had been responsible for mentally *composing* as well as physically *writing* a text, workers in the mechanized office were assigned limited functions as stenographers (who captured an executive's spoken words in shorthand) and typists (who mechanically transcribed such words). The clerk's editorial role diminished as managers split the making of documents into two distinct phases: conception and production. The new system, which borrowed the division of labor from modern factories, saved the high-cost time and effort of managers, while a lower-paid crew of clerical workers generated a huge volume of legible, uniform documents.[3]

In addition to accepting low wages, women offered a number of attractive qualities to employers, including their perceived docility and agility, their willingness to perform routine work, and their lack of career ambitions. Prior to the 1950s, native-born white women typically entered the work force for a brief period before marrying; this pattern discouraged them from expecting the same opportunities for advancement and benefits as men of their class. As historian Elyce Rotella has explained, the routinized modern office that emerged in the late nineteenth century needed large numbers of workers with general skills—transferable to any business—rather than specific skills acquired in relation to a given company. The generically qualified typist or stenographer could be trained in a high school business course or commercial school; the firm that hired her, having invested minimally in her training, thus could take full advantage of both the low wages commanded by women and the rapid turnover associated with their work.

"Between the 1870s and the 1890s, women's entrance into clerical positions posed a direct challenge to the commonly held belief that not only was the office a male space, but also that all sorts of urban settings—elevators, street cars, restaurants, boardinghouses—were inappropriate to women. Women's entrance into these places set in motion a redefinition of women's sphere within the world of work and the city that continued throughout the twentieth century."

Lisa M. Fine, *The Souls of the Skyscraper*, 1990.

In the 1910s and 1920s, the female office worker figured in popular literature and film as a new social type, an adventurer in the urban wilderness—the "flapper" of the 1920s often was a typist.[4] By the 1930s, as historian Mary Kathleen Benét has written, the female clerical force was a familiar cultural fact: "the real novelty had gone from the working girl, and in any description of the office world, she was simply there—as irrevocable and uninteresting as the desks and the telephones." Because typing, stenography, and switchboard operating were thoroughly feminized, women were not pressured to give up these jobs to men during the Depression; many married women with unemployed husbands sought work in offices in the 1930s.

During World War II, women occupied male-defined jobs both in offices and in factories; although they were forced to surrender most of the Rosie-the-Riveter factory positions to returning vets after 1945, women were able to keep many of the lower-paying office jobs they had claimed during the war, including bookkeeping, which has become increasingly feminized since 1950. With the accelerating demand for clerical workers in the 1950s and 1960s, more married women, older women, and women from diverse ethnic and racial backgrounds pursued office jobs; meanwhile, the wages of clerical employees relative to other women workers gradually declined. While in 1890 a female typist earned 1.8 times as much as a female factory worker, this gap diminished between 1900 and 1930, as wages evened out across feminized occupations in teaching, manufacturing, and retail. Since World War II, routine clerical positions have paid much less than factory jobs.

Thus high wages have not been the main incentive for women to become clerical workers. As a site of cultural prestige, the office has been seen as a more appropriate setting than the factory or store for middle-class women; it can serve, in fact, to endow its occupants with a middle-class status. The design of business machines and their environments has shaped and expressed the social meaning of office work. Design has helped articulate the differences between employees occupying various levels of an organization and has linked the language of the office to other institutional vocabularies, such as the home and the factory. Design has molded the psychological, physical, and symbolic value of work in modern offices.[5]

Vertical filing is an information technology central to the modern office. Introduced in 1893, vertical filing organizes material related to a given subject in a flat paper folder that can be easily located, removed, or expanded. The vertical file replaced awkward copy books, flat files, and letter boxes, which store documents in the order they are received. Carlene Stephens and Steven Lubar have called the vertical file the informational analogue to the skyscraper. The catalogue illustration ABOVE, *c. 1923, pictures a dramatic cityscape through the office window. The ad for Corry Jamestown filing cabinets* BELOW, *1966, compares a secretary with her furniture. Warshaw Collection, Smithsonian Institution.*

In 1868 Christopher Latham Sholes, Carlos Glidden, and Samuel Soule registered the first of a series of patents that would result in a commercially viable typewriter three years later. Remington, a gun manufacturer, mass-produced typewriters from 1874 onward; sales exploded in the 1880s, as typewriters—and female typists—became accepted office inhabitants.[6] Most early typewriters had an overtly technological character, as seen in the open architecture of the 1882 Caligraph and the 1907 Remington machines ABOVE (Warshaw Collection, Smithsonian Institution).

The Noiseless, TOP CENTER, was introduced in 1917 after more than a decade of development; it was engineered to operate by pressure rather than by hammering; a sweeping facade conceals the bank of keys (Warshaw Collection). The 1935 Royal shown BOTTOM CENTER is part of a series of standard models initiated in 1923; with each update, the company covered more of the machine's working parts inside a metal shell. While the enclosure is nearly complete in the model shown here, glazed windows in the sides of the machine expose its inner workings.

In the 1930s and 1940s, designers enhanced the engineered rationality of the typewriter with streamlined styling, as seen in the Underwoods ABOVE RIGHT, 1940 and 1947. The company promoted the machine TOP RIGHT as "styled in the modern trend" with a "completely sealed back" (Warshaw Collection).

ABOVE *During World War II, Durez Plastics proposed this experimental design by Dave Chapman as the answer to the question of "How the future will look to your secretary," predicting the rising use of molded plastic, horizontal styling, and electric power in typewriters.*

"It would be difficult to imagine the office without typewriters, telephones, and filing cabinets....They have been central to the definition of what a secretary *is*, and to the construction of the boss/secretary relationship."

Rosemary Pringle, *Secretaries Talk*, 1988.

IBM introduced the first successful electric typewriter in the U.S. in 1935. The colorful, curvaceous Executive AA, TOP LEFT, was marketed from 1946 through the late 1950s. In the 1959 machine at LEFT, designed by Eliot Noyes, a graphically framed keyboard is cut into a low, continuous body. Noyes described his 1961 Selectric, TOP RIGHT, as a design that expresses the disappearance of the movable carriage, made possible by the "golf ball" element: "The shape which evolved is...like that of a large, smooth stone, with scooped out areas for the keyboard and platen."[7] IBM's design philosophy helped define the office as a humane, middle-class place with its own visual language.

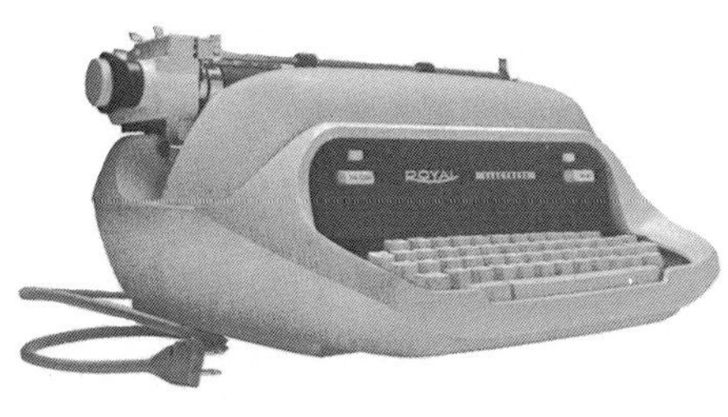

"She [the secretary] likes the sculptured beauty of the Electress. Its quietness, its colors, the crispness of the work it turns out, and its size: full-sized, but not bulky."

Royal brochure, c. 1962.

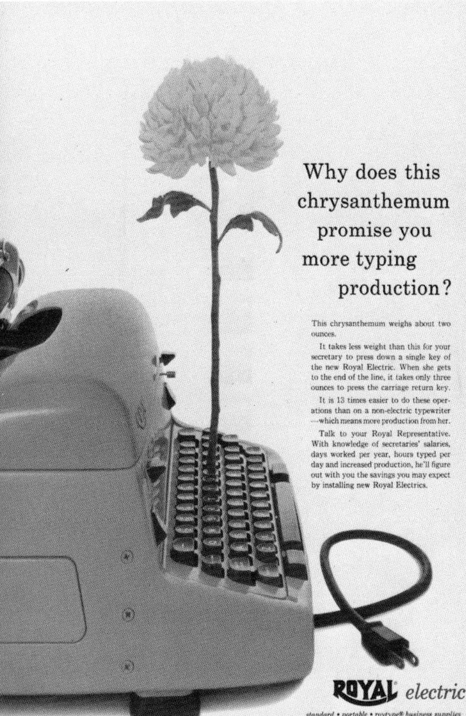

Beginning in the early 1950s, Royal advertised electric typewriters whose forms and colors were designed to minimize the industrial associations of the office and to appeal to female clerical workers, as seen in the 1956 pink machine BOTTOM LEFT. Royal compared its smooth, enclosed typewriter to contemporary fashion in the 1951 ad BELOW RIGHT, juxtaposing a woman in a "New Look" suit with a smartly designed machine.[8] The angular Royal ABOVE LEFT, c. 1961, and the biomorphic Electress ABOVE RIGHT, 1962, represent two extremes in high-style typewriter design. The word-processing terminals of the 1970s emulated the model of the typewriter as a continuous object by treating the keyboard and video screen as a single organism. In the late 1970s, the keyboard split off from the video screen, becoming a distinct unit within a dispersed system of devices.

Certainly, you choose the finest...

ROYAL Electric Typewriter

Utilitarian things are extensions of the biological body—or what Le Corbusier called "human limb-objects" in his modernist manifesto *The Decorative Art of Today* (1925).[9] Corbusier's book presents vernacular office environments as the basis for a new aesthetic for design. In contrast with works of fine art, which are unique expressions of individual taste, "human limb-objects" such as filing cabinets, steel desks, and typewriters reflect, in Corbusier's view, universal functions. Although his office scenarios are uninhabited by human beings, commercial representations of typewriters since the 1880s routinely have been animated by the presence of the female hand—the "limb" extended by the typewriter is prototypically feminine.

The modern boss/secretary relationship is structured by such differences as masculine/feminine and active/passive. Machines mediate these relationships, standing between male decision-making and female service. As sociologist Rosemary Pringle has pointed out, the very notion of "secretary" is cloaked in sexual innuendo; the occupation has no absolute definition in terms of duties or responsibilities, but rather is identified tacitly by its gender (female) and its machines (typewriters and telephones).

With the rise of the personal computer, the keyboard began to lose its association with "women's work" and the female body. A 1982 report on office automation, written at the dawn of the "desktop" era, predicted—inaccurately—that male executives would never agree to use computers unless they could talk into them directly, as if the machines were secretaries or dictaphones.[10] Young men now are encouraged to learn touch-typing in high school, enabling them to operate computer keyboards not only as managers and technicians but as secretaries and "temps." Although "boss" and "secretary" have become less gender dependent positions, 99 percent of secretaries in 1990 were female.[11]

ABOVE *These postcards, c. 1910, reflect the erotic mythology of the office that had emerged by the turn of the century, when popular postcards portrayed female clerks in love triangles composed of a man, a woman, and a typewriter. As the wedge that had opened up this male domain of commerce to women, the typewriter was a crucial link in the office romance.*

"Both secretaries and technology appear as men's possessions, a measure of their worth, the objects as well as the basis of men's power and control. The secretaries are there to operate men's machines and to service men—in ways that are, by implication, rather intimate."

Rosemary Pringle, *Secretaries Talk*, 1988.

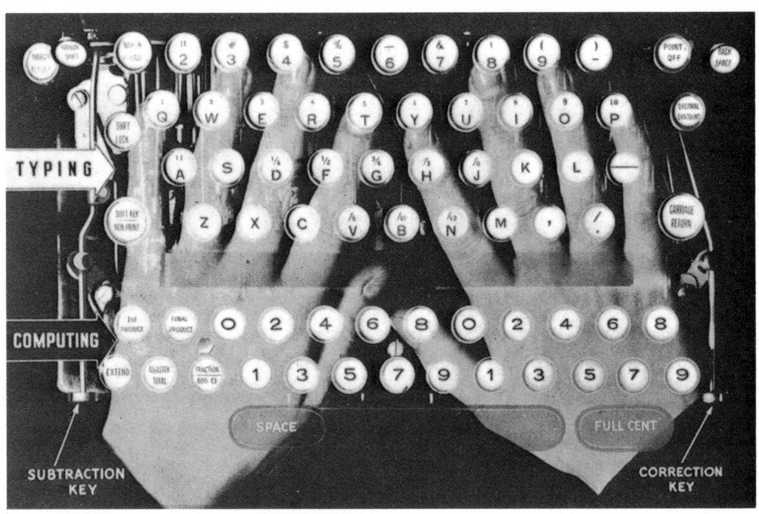

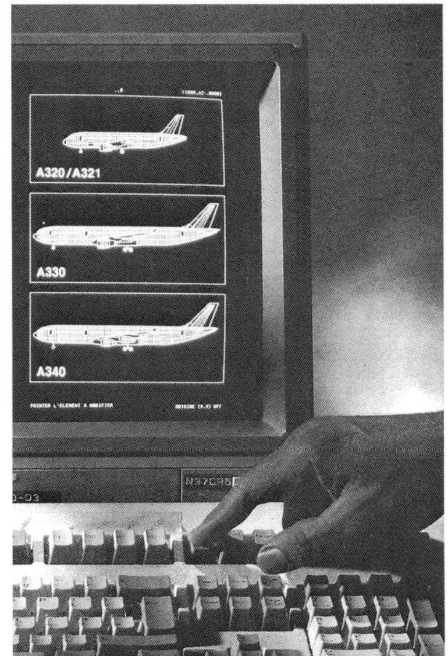

ABOVE LEFT *This photomontage renders the hands of the female typist transparent to the keyboard. Warshaw Collection, Smithsonian Institution.*
ABOVE RIGHT *An advertising photo for Victor Typewriters juxtaposes flowing feminine garments with the hard, open structure of a machine. Warshaw Collection, Smithsonian Institution.*

LEFT *Despite the rise in the use of computers by men since the mid 1980s, conjunctions of the male hand and the keyboard remain rare in advertising. This 1990 ad for Airbus Industrie depicts male computer use in the context of high-tech engineering and push-button control rather than mere typing.*

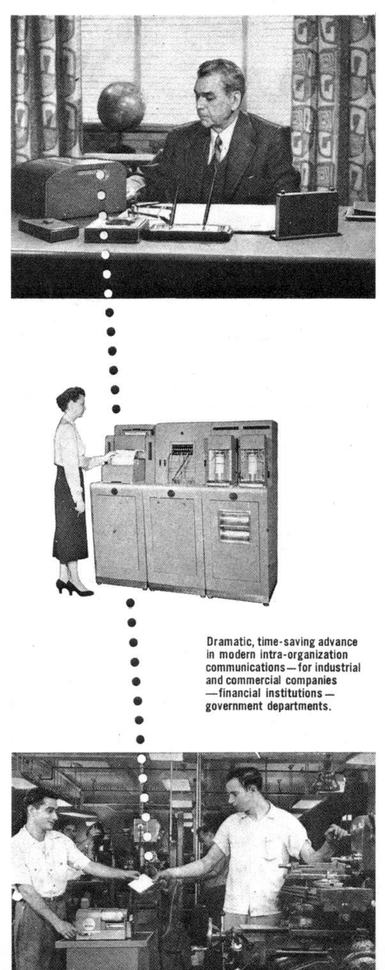

RIGHT *The female body typically is portrayed as an interface with communications technologies, from typewriters (IBM, c. 1956) to fax machines (Western Union, 1953). While men appear to be active producers and users of information, women are a link between them; they are human extensions of the machine.*

ABOVE *In the sun-filled atrium at the center of Frank Lloyd Wright's 1906 Larkin Building, a row of female clerks is flanked by male executives. The clerks' chairs are attached to their desks. The majority of the Larkin Building's clerical workers were female. Courtesy Buffalo and Erie County Historical Society.*

BELOW *In contrast to the Larkin Building's clerical furniture, the chairs for executives glide on castors. The furniture was designed by Wright and manufactured by Van Dorn Iron Works. Courtesy Metropolitan Museum of Art.*

In the period when women began entering clerical occupations, the physical nature of offices was changing. While the traditional office had been a loose amalgam of domestic and commercial idioms, the introduction of machines and the division of clerical work into discrete tasks linked the office to the modern factory. The scientific management movement in the early twentieth century made explicit the link between the office and the factory. The management theorist Frederick W. Taylor had sought to maximize the efficiency of factory workers by rationalizing the production process into a series of repeatable steps. Taylor's ideas were applied to the office in the 1910s and 1920s, by efficiency experts who sought to rationalize bureaucratic procedures.[12]

Frank Lloyd Wright's Larkin Building, which opened in 1906, became a textbook model for the scientific office.[13] The Larkin Soap Company, a mail-order business, employed over a thousand female clerical workers to process the huge volume of paper flowing in and out of its headquarters. From inspirational texts painted on the walls to furniture that restricted the workers' movements, Wright's design program sought to promote the moral virtue and physical productivity of its inhabitants. To complement the building's advanced communications equipment—telephones, typewriters, graphophones, and built-in filing cabinets—Wright designed desks and chairs that emulate the formal language of the machine. The seats of his clerical furniture are attached to massive metal desks on cantilevered arms; by limiting the user's mobility, the design aimed to heighten her efficiency. In contrast to the Larkin Building's clerical seating, the chairs designed for executives rest on wheels that encourage motion. Plain metal construction became standard issue for secretarial desks in the early twentieth century, while executive offices employed more luxurious domestic styles and materials.

RIGHT Donald Deskey Associates designed a family of office furnishings for Globe-Wernicke, c. 1954. This time-motion photo, from the cover of a trade catalogue, draws on the vocabulary of scientific management studies to promote the efficiency of the L-shaped desk. Deskey Archive, Cooper-Hewitt, National Museum of Design.

ABOVE Receptionist's desk from George Nelson's Executive Office Group. This 1957 ad presents the desk with a "cheerful chair" by Charles Eames. Courtesy Herman Miller Archives.

In the decades following World War II, some managers and designers sought to erase the visual link between factories and offices in favor of a corporate design idiom that promotes physical and psychological comfort and emphasizes the unified image of an institution over the relative status of its employees. George Nelson's Executive Office Group of 1948, manufactured by Herman Miller Inc., is a system of desks and storage units designed to accommodate the work needs of office employees at every level—the choice of chair and the presence of a typewriter might be the mark of difference between a secretarial work station and an executive suite.[14] Several modular office systems were available in the early 1950s, which included visually coordinated desks as well as room dividers for articulating vast clerical "bullpens" into semi-private spaces. This new approach was motivated in part by the need to raise the morale of female clerical workers in the burgeoning corporate offices of the 1950s. The office was reconceived as a comfortable place whose high-status environment could help compensate for the low wages characteristic of female-dominated occupations.[15]

"The office that designers are now asked to contrive...is expected to be a civilized environment—more civilized, indeed, than many of its occupants enjoy in their own homes....The office is called upon to be both an outpost and a refuge, where effort and relaxation need not be in conflict."
Eric Larrabee, "The Cult of Work," 1954.

"It would not be surprising to discover that a major cause of alienation from the work place is the place itself." Robert Propst, "Process Aesthetic," 1974.

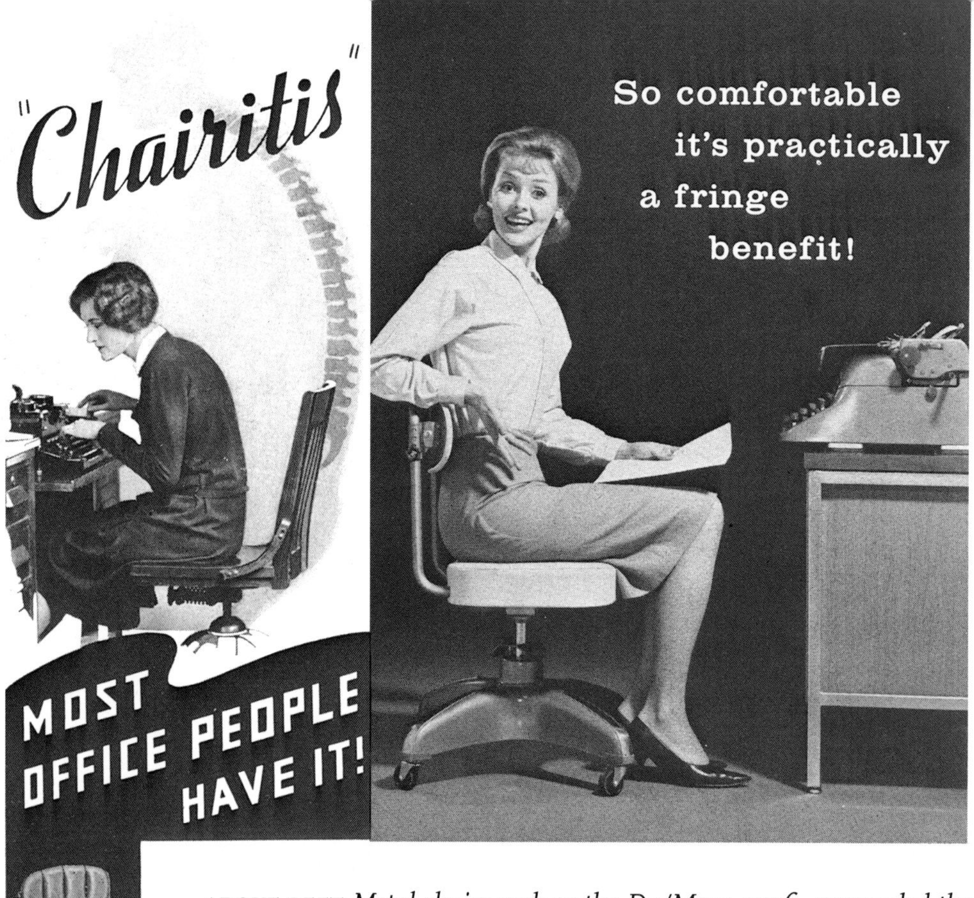

LEFT This ad for Cosco shows that healthy furniture was still considered a privilege, not a right, in 1962.
BELOW The Cosco line includes a throne-like executive chair and a small-backed, armless secretarial chair.

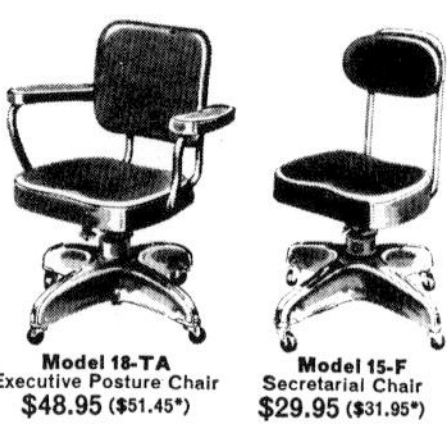

For clerical use the No. 590 Air-Duct is the latest and finest development.

ABOVE LEFT Metal chairs such as the Do/More, 1936, superseded the wooden swivel chair in the early twentieth century.
BELOW LEFT The adjustable wooden swivel chair was invented in 1853; shown here is a typical example from the 1890s, with different sizes for different workers. Warshaw Collection, Smithsonian Institution.
BELOW RIGHT Modern office furniture often reflects assumptions about the physical differences between men (regal and massive) and women (curvy and diminutive), as seen in this family of office chairs. Art Metal, 1967.

"Smallness is what feminism strives against, the smallness that women confront everywhere...women's spaces are smaller than those of men, often inadequate, without privacy. Furniture designers distinguish between a man's and a woman's chair, because women don't spread out like men...."

Sallie Tisdale, "The Weight that Women Carry," 1993.

Unlike the typewriter, the dictaphone was designed and marketed for use by executives. Advocates of scientific management promoted dictaphones as a way to further atomize the production of business communications—because a manager speaking into a recording device is not using the services of a stenographer, she can spend more time typing. Many ads have pictured the dictaphone as a mechanical substitute for the worker. Despite the push, however, by efficiency experts to replace multi-functional secretaries with dictaphones and typing pools, executives often have resisted relinquishing their personal assistants, who are a sign of status as well as a source of consistent, customized help. Likewise, executive secretaries pride themselves on the specialized knowledge and range of skills involved in working with one "boss." Much of the craft and pleasure of office work lies in human interaction.

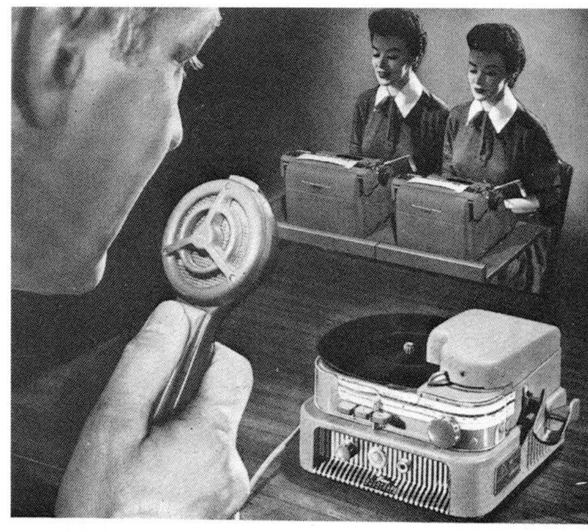

ABOVE *This dictaphone ad claims to double the body of the secretary. Audophone, 1952.*

The 1957 film *The Desk Set*, starring Katherine Hepburn and Spencer Tracy, chronicles the struggle between an office manager and an efficiency expert who hopes to replace Hepburn's all-female staff with a computer named Erniac (LEFT). The film, which ends with the self-destruction of the machine, reflects women's well-founded fears about the technological obsolescence of their jobs.[16] Although female-dominated clerical occupations such as data entry and switchboard operating tend to be low-paying, they are crucial to the economic survival of many women.

LEFT *Office automation has been promoted to businesses as a means to transfer specialized knowledge from the mind of the worker to the apparatus of the company. This 1967 ad for an accounting system shows pregnant "Alice" leaving work after her baby shower, taking valuable information with her; the ad reinforces the myth of the transient female office worker.*

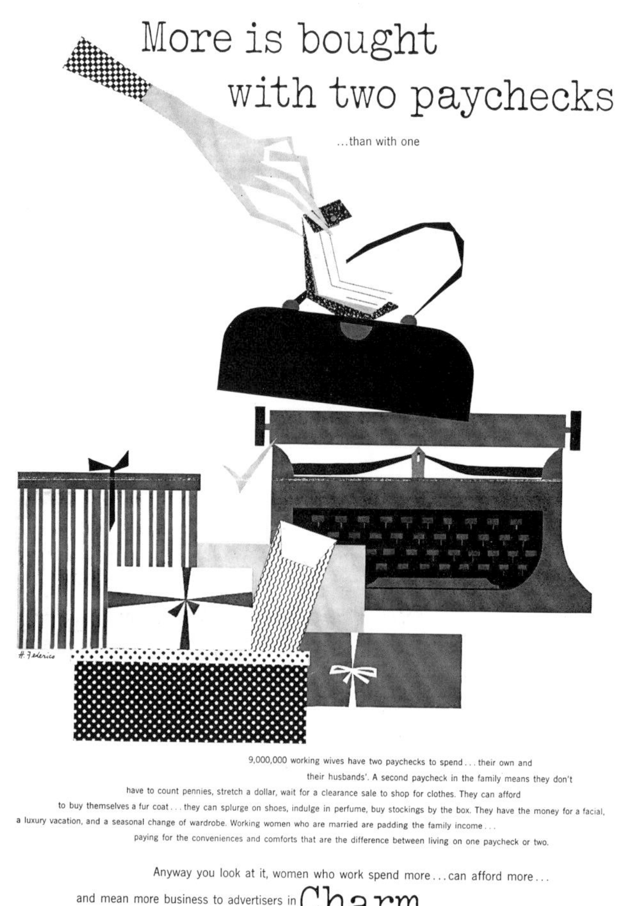

Beginning in 1944, editor Helen Valentine, art director Cipe Pineles, and promotion director Estelle Ellis built *Charm* into the first magazine directed at working women. Previously, the same team had helped invent the teenage market at *Seventeen*. The ads here are from a direct mail campaign created by Ellis and designer Helen Federico, which aimed to convince advertisers that working women are a vital market force. Federico's modernist collages and photograms represent not workers, but a world of objects. In 1951 Ellis commissioned one of the first market surveys of working women, which charts the earnings spent by women in shoes, stockings, cosmetics and other high-status items worn in the office. [17]

LEFT *This photo from an article in* Saturday Evening Post, *1961, about the scarcity of good secretaries features the startling presence of a baby in a corporate office. The caption explains that the secretary is caring for her boss's baby while his wife visits a doctor.*

Among the challenges facing designers and workers in offices today is to begin resolving the conflict between the home and places of employment. The current crises in child care and health care suggest the need to extend the values of nurturing—associated with women and the domestic sphere—to offices and other spaces where people work for money. Both men and women would benefit from achieving widespread recognition of the social and economic value of the labor performed at home, and establishing the work site as a legitimate place for the continuation of care-giving responsibilities.

The rise of "telecommuting" in the last decade, made possible by the proliferation of personal computers, fax machines, and electronic networks, is one phenomenon that is challenging the boundaries between home and office.[18] The implications are especially important for women, for whom the conflict between home and work has weighed heaviest. The emerging "electronic cottage" holds potential dangers as well as advantages for workers, threatening a return to exploitative, unregulated piecework. The merging of home and office technologies also threatens to enable the workday to expand indefinitely, as workers and work become constantly available. Despite its drawbacks, however, working at home has economic, ecological, and personal benefits that have made it a growing business trend, and an important target for design thinking.

ABOVE *Today, fax machines are designed as domestic appliances, as appropriate to the kitchen counter as a toaster or a blender. Courtesy Muratec, 1992.*

> "The home, workplace, market, public arena, the body itself—all can be dispersed and interfaced in nearly infinite, polymorphous ways, with large consequences for women and others...."
>
> Donna Haraway, "A Cyborg Manifesto," 1991.

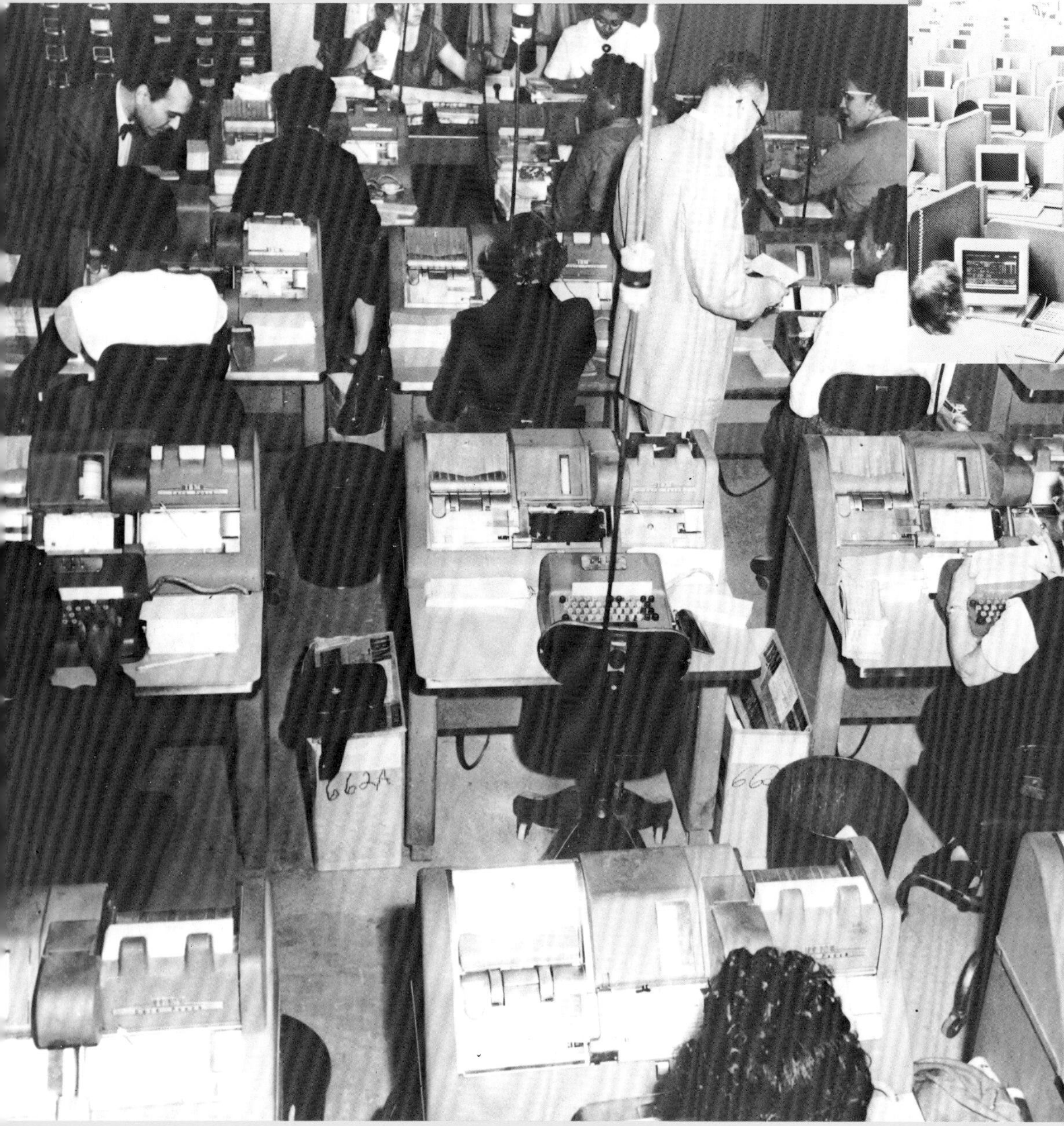

ABOVE CENTER *The introduction of computers in the late 1940s resulted in numerous low-paying data entry jobs in which the computer keyboard inherited the feminized status of the typewriter. Photo, c. 1956, New-York Historical Society, New York.*

ABOVE RIGHT *Today, jobs combining telephone and data entry work form a "pink collar ghetto." Behind the glamorous set of the Home Shopping Club is a sea of work stations. David Graham/Black Star, 1993.*

RIGHT *Seiko's "Receptor" is a paging device that displays a caller's phone number or the message "call home" or "call office." The receptor is made in two styles: a wrist watch worn primarily by men, and a pocket device created for women that resembles a cosmetic compact. Women, children, and young adults recently have become a major market for pagers, which were formerly associated chiefly with professional communications. Mothers commonly use pagers to keep in touch with their children. Seiko, 1993.*

LEFT *1945, New-York Historical Society, New York. Bagoe Collection.*

BELOW *Two women talk to each other from their homes in a 1961 AT&T advertising photo.*

We work, live, and love in a world populated with machines that offer us economic, emotional, and erotic opportunities as well as restrictions and false promises. One of the goals of a feminist analysis of design is to reveal the cultural uses and meanings of the manufactured world. Reading the social text of the designed environment is a step toward achieving power and choice in daily life.

NOTES

Sex Objects

1. On design, streamlining, and the machine, see Richard Guy Wilson, Dianne Pilgrim, and Dickran Tashjian, *The Machine Age in America, 1918–1941* (New York: Brooklyn Museum, 1986). See also Donald J. Bush, *The Streamlined Decade* (New York: George Braziller, 1975) and Jeffrey L. Meikle, *Twentieth Century Limited: Industrial Design in America, 1925–1939* (Philadelphia: Temple University Press, 1979). On car design, see Karal Ann Marling, "America's Love Affair with the Automobile in the Television Age," *Design Quarterly* 146 (1989): 5–19.

2. J. Gordon Lippincott asserts the primacy of the female consumer in *Design for Business* (Chicago: Paul Theobold, 1947).

3. For a general history of working women, see Alice Kessler-Harris, *Out to Work: A History of Wage-Earning Women in the United States* (New York: Oxford University Press, 1982).

4. Betty Friedan revived the women's movement with *The Feminine Mystique* (New York: Dell Publishing, 1963).

5. Marshall McLuhan helped found modern media studies with his book *The Mechanical Bride: Folklore of Modern Man* (New York: Vanguard Press, 1951).

6. On cultural studies, see Daniel Miller, *Material Culture and Mass Consumption* (Oxford: Basil Blackwell, 1987).

7. On commodity fetishism, see Karl Marx, *Capital*, Vol. I (New York: International Publishers, 1966), 35–41, 71–79; and Wolfgang Fritz Haug, *Commodity Aesthetics, Ideology, and Culture* (New York: International General, 1987).

8. On the sexual fetish, see Sigmund Freud, "Fetishism," *Sexuality and the Psychology of Love* (New York: Collier Books, 1963), 214–19.

9. Gayle Rubin analyzes the "sex/gender" system in relation to anthropology and psychoanalysis in "The Traffic in Women: Notes on the Political Economy of Sex," *Toward an Anthropology of Women*, ed. Rayna Rapp Reiter (New York: Monthly Review, 1975), 157–210.

10. Feminist histories of technology include Ruth Schwartz Cowan, *More Work for Mother: The Ironies of Household Technology from the Open Hearth to the Microwave* (New York: Basic Books, 1983); Christina Hardyment, *From Mangle to Microwave: The Mechanization of Household Work* (Cambridge: Polity Press, 1988); and Susan Strasser, *Never Done: A History of American Housework* (New York: Pantheon, 1982).

Design history is considered from a feminist viewpoint in Dolores Hayden, *The Grand Domestic Revolution* (Cambridge: MIT Press, 1981) and *Redesigning the American Dream: The Future of Housing, Work, and Family* (New York: W. W. Norton, 1984); Adrian Forty, *Objects of Desire* (New York: Pantheon, 1986); and Penny Sparke, *Electrical Appliances: Twentieth-Century Design* (New York: E. P. Dutton, 1987).

Critical overviews of feminist approaches to design history include Judy Attfield, "FORM/female follows FUNCTION/male: Feminist Critiques of Design," in *Design History and the History of Design*, ed. John A. Walker (London: Pluto Press, 1989), 199–235; Cheryl Buckley, "Made in Patriarchy: Towards a Feminist Analysis of Women and Design," *Design Issues* 3 (1987): 3–15; and Barbara Oldershaw, "Developing a Feminist Critique of Architecture," *Design Book Review* 25 (Summer 1992): 7–15. See also *Sexuality and Space*, ed. Beatriz Colomina (New York: Princeton Architectural Press, 1992).

Love, Leisure, and Laundry

1. For critical overviews of the literature on housework and technology, see Christine E. Bose, Philip L. Bereano, and Mary Molloy, "Household Technology and the Social Construction of Housework," *Technology and Culture* 25 (January 1984): 53–82; and Nona Glazer-Malbin, "Housework," *Signs* 1 (1976): 905–22.

2. The history of the commercial laundry industry is chronicled in Fred DeArmond, *The Laundry Industry* (New York: Harper and Brothers, 1950). Sheila Lewenhak finds similar situations internationally, where manufacturers of home appliances discouraged the development of communal facilities; see *The Revaluation of Women's Work* (London: Croom Helm, 1988), 70–87.

3. Members of the progressive home economics movement commonly endorsed centralized commercial laundry services. See William C. Rogers, "Commercial Laundries in New York City," *Journal of Home Economics* 5, no. 1 (February 1913): 44–47; and Mary Avery White, "The Removal of Laundry Work from the Home," *American Kitchen* 9, no. 6 (September 1898): 203–207.

4. A 1917 article advocating commercial laundries denigrates the "ignorant washerwoman" in favor of "professional laundrymen"; see "The Technology of the Washroom," *Scientific American* 116 (5 May 1917): 445. Most employees in commercial establishments were women, supervised by male foremen.

5. Juliet B. Schor analyzes the economics of housework in *The Overworked American: The Unexpected Decline of Leisure* (New York: Basic Books, 1992).

6. Studies of domestic service include David Katzman,

Seven Days a Week: Women and Domestic Service in Industrializing America (Urbana: University of Illinois Press, 1978); Evelyn Nakano Glenn, *Issei, Nisei, War Bride: Three Generations of Japanese American Women in Domestic Service* (Philadelphia: Temple University Press, 1986), and Phyllis Palmer, *Domesticity and Dirt: Housewives and Domestic Servants in the United States, 1920–1945* (Philadelphia: Temple University Press, 1984). Mary Romero focuses on the experience of Chicanas in *Maid in the USA* (New York: Routledge, 1992).

7. On domestic time use, see Joann Vanek, "Household Technology and Social Status: Rising Living Standards and Residence Differences in Housework," *Technology and Culture* 19 (1978): 361–75.

8. Vanek's thesis is further confirmed in Catherine White Berheide et al., "Household Work in the Suburbs: The Job and Its Participants," *Pacific Sociological Review* 19 (October 1976): 491–518.

9. The decline of housekeeping is reported in "Bless the Mess and Drop the Mop: The Decline of Housekeeping," *New York Times* (10 April 1993): A1, A13.

10. Arlie Hochschild takes a case-study approach to housework in *The Second Shift* (New York: Avon, 1989).

11. Siegfried Giedion's *Mechanization Takes Command* remains the most ambitious study of the technology and design of household equipment (New York: Oxford University Press, 1948). In addition to the discussion of laundry in Cowan, Hardyment, Sparke, and Strasser, see "Domestic Hardware," *Design* 334 (October 1976): 26–33; Enrico Morteo, "Questioni di Design: Le Lavatrici Come Esempio," *Domus* 706 (June 1989): 71–79; "Post-War Home Appliances Challenge Designer and Manufacturer Alike," *Ceramic Industry* 40 (June 1943): 45–47; and "Wringer Washing Machines," *Industrial Design* (September 1960): 92–93.

12. On the history of Maytag, see *An American Classic* (Newton, Iowa: Maytag, n.d.). Harold van Doren discusses streamlining and its application to the Maytag, in *Industrial Design: A Practical Guide* (New York: McGraw-Hill, 1940).

13. Brook Stevens claims to have put the first door on an electric drier in 1936; see Isabel Wilkerson, "The Man Who Put Form on Your Harley, Color in Your Kitchen," *New York Times* (11 July 1991): B1, B5.

14. The Bendix Duomatic is discussed in "Two-in-One," *House and Home* 3 (January 1953): 158.

15. Laundry planning is compared to kitchen planning in "Laundries," *House and Garden* 73 (March 1938): 36–37; "Planning—Laundries," *American Builder and Building Age* 72 (July 1950): 104; and numerous other articles. On the emergence of the modern kitchen, see Ellen Lupton and J. Abbott Miller, *The Bathroom, the Kitchen, and the Aesthetics of Waste* (New York: Princeton Architectural Press, 1992).

16. On the recent appliance business, see *Major Appliance Industry Facts Book* (Chicago: National Association of Home Appliances, 1987).

17. On the history of irons, see Esther S. Berney, *A Collector's Guide to Pressing Irons and Trivets* (New York: Crown Publishers, 1977); and Earl Lifshey, *The Housewares Story: A History of the American Housewares Industry* (Chicago: National Housewares Manufacturers Association, 1973). Larry Salomon's video *The Culture of Objects: Irons* (Chicago: University of Illinois at Chicago) was useful for this study.

18. On the Lady Light iron, see "Small Appliance Marketing: Thermoplastics Tackle a Hot Product," *Plastics World* 38 (September 1980): 83–85.

19. *Good Housekeeping* devoted its May 1958 issue to wash and wear fabrics and cleaning products. See also "In Men's Suits, Automatic Wash and Wear," *American Fabrics* 89 (Winter 1957): 74.

20. Michael Thompson analyzes the unstable worth of objects in *Rubbish Theory: The Creation and Destruction of Value* (New York: Oxford University Press, 1979).

1. Henry Dreyfuss discusses the rational philosophy behind his designs for telephones and other objects in *Designing for People* (New York: Viking, 1955).

2. Lana Rakow evaluates the history of telephone use from a feminist perspective in *Gender on the Line: Women, the Telephone, and Community Life* (Urbana: University of Illinois Press, 1992), "Women and the Telephone: The Gendering of a Communications Technology," in *Technology and Women's Voices: Keeping in Touch*, ed. Cheris Kramarae (New York: Routledge and Kegan Paul, 1988), 207–29. See also Rakow and Vija Navarro, "Remote Mothering and the Parallel Shift: Women Meet the Cellular Telephone," *Critical Studies in Mass Communication* 10 (1993): 144-57.

The idea that women are "naturally" suited to telephone work is presented as a matter of fact in H. M. Boettinger, *The Telephone Book: Bell, Watson, and American Life, 1876–1976* (Croton-on-Hudson, NY: Riverwood Publishers, Ltd., 1977). Boettinger reports, "Few devices are so well matched [as the telephone] to the particular needs and style of women. The instrument seems particularly suited to their voice range and timbre" (p.15).

The feminization of the telephone operator is studied by Michèle Martin in *Hello Central? Gender, Technology, and Culture in the Formation of Telephone Systems* (Montreal: McGill-Queen's University Press, 1991) and "'Rulers of the Wires'? Women's Contribution to the Structure of a Means of Communication," *The Journal of Communication Inquiry* 12 (Summer 1988): 89–103.

Advertising created by N. W. Ayer for AT&T is housed at the Center for Advertising History, National Museum of American History, Smithsonian Institution.

3. On electronic monitoring, see *Stories of Mistrust and Manipulation: The Electronic Monitoring of the American Workforce* (Cleveland: 9 to 5, 1990).

4. On the wage difference between unionized and nonunionized telephone operators and service representatives, see "High-Tech and Low-Wage: Labor Costs at Sprint Long Distance" (Washington, D.C.: Communications Workers of America, 1993); prepared for the Committee on Government Operations, U.S. House of Representatives.

5. Marshall McLuhan's book *Understanding Media* includes chapters on the telephone and the typewriter (New York: Signet Books, 1964), 227–40. Donald Ball develops McLuhan's argument that the telephone can be used to level social hierarchies in "Toward a Sociology of Telephones and Telephoners," *Sociology and Everyday Life*, ed. Marcello Truzzi (Englewood Cliffs, New Jersey: Prentice-Hall, 1968), 59–74. Sidney Aronson credits the telephone with strengthening personal relationships in vast electronic neighborhoods in "The Sociology of the Telephone," *Inter/Media: Interpersonal Communication in a Media World*, ed. Gary Gumpert (New York: Oxford University Press, 1982), 272–83. Avital Ronell analyses the telephone call as a philosophical speech act in *The Telephone Book: Technology, Schizophrenia, Electric Speech* (Lincoln: University of Nebraska Press, 1989). Amy Lawrence talks about the telephone in *Echo and Narcissus: Women's Voices in Classical Hollywood Cinema* (Berkeley: University of California Press, 1991).

6. On the history of the telephone as an object, see P. J. Povey and R. A. J. Earl, *Vintage Telephones of the World* (London: Peter Peregrinus Ltd., 1988) and Michael Sorkin, "Just a Phone Call Away," *Industrial Design* (March/April 1983): 24–39.

7. The industrial designer Don Wallance includes a chapter on telephone design in *Shaping America's Products* (New York: Reinhold Publishing, 1956), 30–40.

8. In his book *The Telephone: The First Hundred Years* (New York: Harper and Row, 1975, 1976), John Brooks describes the shift at AT&T in the late 1950s toward rethinking the telephone as a consumer product.

9. On recent developments, see Anthony Ramirez, "Rethinking the Plain Old Telephone," *New York Times* (Sunday, 3 January 1993): Section 3, p.1.

10. Female domestic phone use is studied by Claude S. Fischer in *America Calling: A Social History of the Telephone to 1940* (Berkeley: University of California Press, 1992) and "Gender and the Residential Telephone, 1890–1940: Technologies of Sociability," *Sociological Forum* 3 (1988): 211–33, and Michèle Martin, cited above. Erving Goffman includes images of women "luxuriating in a call" in his visual dictionary of advertising poses, *Gender Advertisements* (New York: Harper and Row, 1976), 68.

1. The "private secretary" continued to be a male-identified position into the twentieth century; see Edward Jones Kilduff, *The Private Secretary: His Duties and Opportunities* (New York: The Century Co., 1916).

2. Histories of clerical work include Mary Kathleen Benét, *The Secretarial Ghetto* (New York: McGraw-Hill Book Company, 1972); Margery W. Davies, *Woman's Place is at the Typewriter: Office Work and Office Workers, 1870–1930* (Philadelphia, 1982); Harry Braverman, *Labor and Monopoly Capital: The Degradation of Work in the Twentieth Century* (New York: Monthly Review Press, 1974), Chapter 15; Lisa M. Fine, *The Souls of the Skyscraper: Female Clerical Workers in Chicago, 1870–1930* (Philadelphia: Temple University Press, 1990); Margaret L. Hedstrom, "Beyond Feminisation: Clerical Workers in the United States from the 1920s through the 1960s," *The White-Blouse Revolution*, ed. Gregory Anderson (Manchester: University of Manchester Press, 1988), 144–65; Rosemary Pringle, *Secretaries Talk: Sexuality, Power, and Work* (New York and London: Verso, 1988); and Elyce Rotella, *From Home to Office: U.S. Women at Work, 1870–1930* (Ann Arbor: UMI Research Press, 1981).

3. The material culture of the early modern office is documented in JoAnne Yates, *Control through Communication: The Rise of System in American Management* (Baltimore: Johns Hopkins University Press, 1989).

4. C. Wright Mills discusses the literature of the "office girl" in his classic study *White Collar: The American Middle Classes* (New York: Oxford University Press, 1951).

5. Adrian Forty's chapter on offices in *Objects of Desire* (New York: Pantheon, 1986) remains the single most compelling interpretation of office design. Other histories include Edward Casson, "The Evolution of Business Machines and Office Equipment," *Art and Industry*

(January 1951): 208–11; Frances Duffy, "Office Buildings and Organisational Change," in *Buildings and Society*, ed. A. D. King (London, 1980); Judy Graf Klein, *The Office Book: Ideas and Designs for Contemporary Work Spaces* (New York: Facts on File, 1982); Lance Knobel, *Office Furniture: Twentieth-Century Design* (New York: E. P. Dutton, 1987); Stephen A. Kurtz, "Anonymous Space," *Progressive Architecture* (November 1969): 93–110; *L'Empire du Bureau, 1900–2000* (Paris: CNAP/Berger-Levrault, 1984); Jeremy Meyerson and Sylvia Katz, *Home Office* (New York: Van Nostrand Reinhold, 1990); and *Steelcase, the First Seventy-Five Years* (Grand Rapids: Steelcase Inc., 1987). On nineteenth-century office furniture, see Camille J. Showalter and Janice Driesbach, eds., *Wooton Patent Desks* (Indiana State Museum and Oakland Museum, 1983). On recent designs for office equipment, see *Good Offices* (Fort Lauderdale, Florida: Arango Design Foundation, 1989).

6. On the history of the typewriter as an object, see Wilfred A. Bleeching, *Century of the Typewriter* (London: Heinemann, 1974); Edward E. Quiring, *The History of the Typewriter in the United States from 1933 through 1977*, Ph. D. dissertation (Grand Forks: University of North Dakota).

7. On the IBM Selectric, see "Carriage Trade," *Industrial Design* 8 (September 1961): 48–49.

8. On the "New Look" as an idiom shifting from fashion to objects, see Leslie Jackson, *The New Look: Design in the Fifties* (New York: Thames and Hudson, 1991).

9. Le Corbusier presents anonymous office spaces as prototypes for modernism in *The Decorative Art of Today*, trans. James Dunnett (Cambridge: MIT Press, 1987).

10. In 1982 Judith Gregory and Karen Nussbaum predicted that executives would never use computer stations unless they could speak to them directly; "Race Against Time: Automation of the Office," *Office: Technology and People* 1 (1982): 197–236.

11. V. Aldrich reports on male typing in "If You Ask Me, Men Have Been Typecast," *Washington Post* (25 April 1991): C5. The demographic pattern of contemporary clerical work is charted in Paula Ries and Anne J. Stone, *The American Woman, 1992–93, A Status Report* (New York: W. W. Norton and Company, 1992).

12. Manifestos of "scientific management" in the office include L. Galloway, *Office Management, Its Principles and Practice* (New York: Ronald Press Company, 1919); and W. H. Leffingwell, *Office Management* (Chicago: A. W. Shaw, 1925). A photo of Frank Lloyd Wright's Larkin Building is the frontispiece of Galloway's book.

13. On the Larkin Building, see Jack Quinan, *Frank Lloyd Wright's Larkin Building: Myth and Fact* (New York and Cambridge: MIT Press, 1987).

A number of feminist studies have looked at the relationship between gender, space, and freedom of movement in offices, homes, neighborhoods, and cities. See Phil Goodall, "Design and Gender," *Block* 9 (1983): 50–61; Linda McDowell, "City and Home: Urban Housing and the Sexual Division of Space," *Sexual Divisions: Patterns and Processes*, ed. Mary Evans and Clare Ungerson (London: Tavistock Publications, 1983), 142–163; and Susana Torre, "Space as Matrix," *Heresies* 3 (1981): 51–52.

14. George Nelson's Executive Office Group is presented in *ABC of Modern Furniture* (Zeeland, Michigan: Herman Miller, n.d.). On George Nelson's and Robert Propst's Action Office, see "The Herman Miller Action Office," *Interiors* (December 1964): 83–87. Propst outlines his theory of the workplace in "Process Aesthetic," *Progressive Architecture* 11 (November 1979): 78–81.

15. Eric Larrabee evaluates modernist office systems in "The Cult of Work: What Is Happening to the Office?" *Industrial Design* 1 (April 1954): 20–31.

16. Roslyn Feldberg and Evelyn Nakano Glenn discuss technological obsolescence in "Technology and Work Degradation: Effects of Office Automation on Women Clerical Workers," in *Machina Ex Dea: Feminist Perspectives on Technology*, ed. Joan Rothschild (New York: Pergamon Press, 1983), 59–75. On technological obsolescence at AT&T, see Sally Hacker, "Sex Stratification, Technology, and Organizational Change: A Longitudinal Case Study of AT&T," *Social Problems* 26 (1979): 539–57.

17. Promotional materials created under Estelle Ellis's direction over a forty-year period are housed at the Center for Advertising History, Archives Center, National Museum of American History, Smithsonian Institution.

18. On the pros and cons of telecommuting, see Eileen Boris and Cynthia Daniels, *Homework: Historical and Contemporary Perspectives on Paid Labor at Home* (Urbana: University of Illinois Press, 1989).

CHRONOLOGY: WOMEN, WORK, AND TECHNOLOGY

1805, first U.S. patent for a washing machine is filed, but industry does not develop until **1850s** (Hardyment, 56).

1844, the telegraph is introduced, enabling the instant transmission of written information (Yates, 22).

1868, Christopher Latham Sholes, Carlos Glidden, and Samuel Soule begin patenting the first commercially viable typewriter (Yates, 39).

1869, a vertical-axis, gyrator-type washing machine is developed for commercial use. It is the basis of the washing machines of the 1930s (Giedion, 551–52).

1870s, electric light becomes a major competitor of gas light (Sparke, 37).

1870, Mary Florence Potts patents a flat iron with a detachable handle (Hardyment, 69).

1870, 52 percent of the female work force is employed in the category "domestic and personal service"; this figure declines to 20 percent by **1920**. During this period of *general* decline in the percentage of women employed in domestic service, the percentage of *women of color* increases: for African-American women, the percentage is 46 percent in **1920**, 35 percent in **1930**, and 60 percent in **1940** (Palmer, 12).

Between **1870** and **1910**, it becomes common for middle-class families to send their laundry out to commercial establishments. In each decade of this 40-year span, the number of women employed in commercial laundries rises between 50 and 100 percent, exceeding by far the population growth (Kessler-Harris, 112).

1876, Alexander Graham Bell invents the telephone. Western Union hires Thomas Edison in **1877** to improve Bell's invention. Western Union sells the patent rights in **1879** to the National Bell Company, which becomes American Telephone and Telegraph in **1885** (Chandler).

1877, the "box telephone" is the first American subscriber's telephone, followed by the desk stand of 1879 and the wall telephone of 1882. Between **1892** and **1914**, a succession of desk stands or "candlestick" phones are introduced (Wallance, 34).

1877–78, the telephone exchange is invented, allowing calls to be routed from one phone to any other phone in the system (Yates, 21).

Between **1881** and **1884**, nearly 18,000 typewriters are sold in the U. S.; only 4,000 had been sold between **1874** and **1878** (Yates, 41).

After the **1880s**, more and more women will begin working for wages, reflecting the shift from an economy based on home production to one based on consumption, and thus an economy of cash (Kessler-Harris, 109).

In **1880**, 73.3 percent of black single women and 35.4 percent of black married women in 7 southern cities work for wages; only 23.8 percent of single women and 7.3 percent of married women work for wages (Kessler-Harris, 123–24).

1882, patent is granted to H. W. Seely of New Jersey for an electric ("carbon arc") iron; it is not a commercial success (Hardyment, 73).

By **1887**, the "Graphophone" is marketed as a machine for recording dictation, employing the technology of Edison's phonograph (Yates, 44–45).

In **1890**, more than 90 percent of women over 30 are married; the vast majority are outside of the paid labor force. In **1890**, the census counts only 3.3 percent of married women as wage-earners; by **1920**, this figure has nearly tripled to 9 percent (Kessler-Harris, 122).

In **1890**, only 35.3 percent of female wage-earners are native-born children of native-born parents; by **1920**, the percent is nearly 44. The more affluent enter the professions, while the less affluent enter clerical work (Kessler-Harris, 119).

1892, R. G. Brown creates a portable telephone handset, combining earpiece, handle, and mouthpiece in a single unit, for use at the central telephone exchange in New York. In Paris a lighter-weight handset is designed for the female operators; it becomes a component of subscribers' phones as well. The handset is not incorporated into subscriber phones in the U. S. until **1927** (Wallance, 33).

By **1902** there are 37,000 female telephone operators in the U.S., as compared to 2,500 male (Benét, 37).

1902, 8 percent of U. S. homes have electricity provided from power stations; by **1948**, the figure is 78 percent (Hardyment, 28).

1904, Hotpoint introduces the first commercially produced electric irons in the U. S. (Hardyment, 73).

1908, the invention of the small electric motor by A. J. Fisher enables the production of effective domestic washing machines and other appliances. Initially, the motors are sold as units separate from the appliances themselves (Hardyment, 63).

1909, Leo Baekeland invents the substance "Bakelite." General Electric uses it for a control knob on an iron in the late **1920s**; it soon becomes popular for handles, replacing wood, and then for the "bodies" of telephones, cameras, and other objects (Sparke, 42).

Between **1910** and **1920**, the number of domestic servants *drops* from 1,851,000 to 1,411,000, while the number of households *rises* from 20.3 million to 24.4 million (Weisman, 92).

1912, the American Beauty electric iron is introduced, the first to be directed at the domestic market (Sparke, 87).

By **1913**, General Electric is marketing irons, toasters, and an electric range for the consumer market; sales do not become signficant until the **1920s** (Sparke, 27).

1918, 24.3 percent of U. S. households are wired for

electricity; in **1925**, 53.2 percent of U.S. homes are wired (Cowan, 1976, 159).

Between **1921** and **1929**, the output of the home appliance industry triples in value (Sparke, 27).

1926, 900,000 washing machines are sold at an average price of 150 dollars; in **1935**, 1.4 million are sold for 60 dollars (Hardyment, 63).

1927, the one-piece handset made of phenolic plastic becomes a feature of subscriber phones in the U. S. (Wallance, 34).

1927, Maytag sells its millionth washer (Sparke, 82).

1927, Americans spend $667 million on household appliances, a 500 percent increase over the **1909** expenditure of $145 million (Cowan, 1976, 159).

1927, inspired by economic recession, Henry Ford adopts General Motors's policy of designing new car models each year. By the end of the **1920s**, stylistic obsolescence is commonplace, and is further encouraged by the Depression in the **1930s** (Sparke, 48).

1929, Bell Labs commissions five "artists" to submit proposals for new telephone designs, focusing on appearance. Among them is Henry Dreyfuss, who had just opened an industrial design office. The collaboration results in the 300 Series of **1937** (Wallance, 35-36).

By **1929**, 11 manufacturers control 85 percent of the home appliance industry in the U. S. (Sparke, 27).

In **1930**, 4.5 million people are counted as unemployed; the number rises to 8 million in **1931**, and 13 million in **1932**—a quarter of the workforce. Women are now encouraged to seek employment, often to support unemployed men. Because female labor is cheaper, it is easier for women to get jobs (Kessler-Harris, 250–51).

1937, a study by *Fortune* magazine reports that "70 percent of the rich, 42 percent of the upper middle class, 14 percent of the lower middle class, and 6 percent of the poor" claim to hire some domestic help (Palmer, 9).

In **1940**, one out of every five working women—two million in all—is a servant. Half of these are black or Hispanic. Servants are among the lowest paid of female workers (Kessler-Harris, 270).

1942, Pearl Harbor brings home the fact that women will be needed for war production. Some industries even provide them with transportation, day care, banking facilities, and other conveniences. "Rosie the Riveter" becomes a popular radio tune (Kessler-Harris, 275–76).

1945 onward, General Electric, Westinghouse, Frigidaire, Sunbeam, Maytag, and Hoover are household words in the U. S. (Sparke, 30).

Between **1946** and **1960**, AT&T's workforce shifts toward male employment: from 69.5 percent female in **1946** to 57.9 percent female in **1960**. The shift reflects a decrease in the lower-skilled jobs (female) and an increase in skilled jobs (male). Technology eliminates clerical and operating jobs, while during the same period jobs increase in management, sales, plant crafts, and business jobs. Between **1958** and **1964**, 80,000 AT&T jobs are eliminated; most of them had been held by women (Hacker, 544).

1950, the 500 Series phone, designed by Henry Dreyfuss, is introduced; development had begun in 1946; design was completed in 1949 (Wallance, 32).

After **1950**, a secretary is at least as likely to be married as single, and her average age rises, despite the myth of the sexy, single, young secretary (Binét, 580).

In **1950**, women constitute 29 percent of the work force; 35 percent in **1965**; 40 percent in **1975**—a percentage increase equal to that of the entire 60-year period prior to **1950**. A third of all women work for wages in **1950**, but only half of them work full-time. By **1975**, more than 70 percent of employed women hold full-time jobs. Most of this growth occurs in the clerical and service sectors (Kessler-Harris, 301).

In **1950**, 21.6 percent of wives work for wages; in **1960**, 30.5 percent do. The rise of two-income families during the **1950s** is linked to consumerism: "Homes and cars, refrigerators and washing machines, telephones and multiple televisions required higher incomes" (Kessler-Harris, 302).

In **1950**, 62 percent of U. S. households have telephones; 78 percent in **1960**; 90 percent in **1970**; and 93 percent in **1980** (Fischer, 259).

1959, AT&T introduces the Princess phone in selected markets, described by industry historian John Brooks as "light and stylishly feminine in design" (Brooks, 266).

1959, AT&T begins developing its electronic switching system (ESS). The first commercial computerized telephone exchange is installed in **1965** (Brooks, 278–79).

By **1960**, nearly 80 percent of wage-earning women work in female-identified occupations, including stenography, typing, nursing, teaching, social work, and health care. By **1960**, the median annual income of women is 60 percent that of men, a fact that reflects their "increasing occupational segregation." The median *drops* to 58 percent in the mid **1960s** (Kessler-Harris, 303–11).

Between **1960** and **1988**, employment in the "service-producing sector" rises 138 percent. Women workers account for more than 75 percent of the increase. In **1960**, less than 20 percent of service-sector employees were women; in **1990**, the percent is more than half. These occupations include domestic service, protective service, teaching, waitressing, nursing, and the wholesale and retail trades (Ries, 330–31).

1961, AT&T introduces Centrex service to businesses, "enabling a large office to maintain its automatic switching exchange and internal numbers to be dialed directly" (Brooks, 266).

1964, the Civil Rights Act is passed, forbidding discrimination on grounds of religion, race, and ethnicity as well as sex (Kessler-Harris, 314).

1960s, appliance design becomes dominated by the "white cube" aesthetic, from stoves to washers and dryers (Sparke 24). The cube aesthetic is inspired not so much by changed marketing demands as by the "high-minded design ideals" of modernism. Black and white "boxes" are ubiquitous by the early **1970s** (Sparke, 55).

1965, AT&T introduces the Trimline, designed by Henry Dreyfuss (Brooks, 266).

In **1965**, only 27 percent of AT&T subscribers were on party lines; the percentage had been 40 in **1960** and 75 in **1950** (Brooks, 267).

1965–66, a national survey finds that working women average 3 hours of housework each day, while men average 17 minutes; women spend 50 minutes a day exclusively with their children, while men spend 12 minutes. Working fathers spend one hour more than their wives watching television, and sleep half an hour longer (Hochschild, 3).

In **1971**, the EEOC investigates sex and race discrimination at AT&T, then the largest private employer in the U. S. In **1972** the government requires AT&T to institute affirmative action plans, opening management programs and plant jobs to women and minorities. During this period, affirmative action put 16,300 men in traditionally female jobs, while only 9,400 women were placed in traditionally male jobs. Between **1972** and **1975**, 36,000 AT&T jobs are eliminated, most of them for operators, lower level clericals, and lower level managers. These jobs are held primarily by women (Hacker).

1974, the Ford Administration files suit against AT&T to break up the Bell monopoly. Divestiture becomes effective in **1984**, at which point people begin owning, rather than leasing, their phones (Fischer, 258).

In **1978**, almost half of all female-headed households in the U.S. are below the poverty line, compared to 5 percent of male-headed households. In **1980**, 73 percent of American households in public housing are headed by women; by the late **1980s**, the percentage is more than 90 percent (Weisman, 105–6).

In **1980**, 32 percent of white women are employed as clerical workers, while only 25 percent of black women are so employed. The numbers for Asian and Hispanic females fall somewhere in between. While women as a whole are over-represented in clerical work, minorities generally are not (Hunt, 50).

Between **1980** and **1990**, women's earnings increased from 64 cents per male dollar to 72 cents per male dollar. Between **1983** and **1990**, men's earnings declined during this period in 6 out of 8 occupational categories, while women's earnings went up slightly. The narrowing of the female-male earnings ratio is thus accountable, in part, to the drop in male earnings. The one area in which men's earnings rose appreciably during the **1980s** was in managerial/professional occupations (Ries, 363).

1985, 70 percent of U. S. households have washing machines, as compared to 73.5 percent in **1960**. 66 percent of households have electric dryers in **1985**, as compared to 17.3 percent in **1960**. 99.9 percent of households have refrigerators in **1985**, as compared to 93.4 percent in **1960** (Major Appliance Industry Facts Book).

1988, 99.1 percent of all secretaries are women, as compared to 97.8 percent in **1970** (9 to 5).

1990, 56 percent of all American women are married and live with their spouses. For white women, the percent is 59; for black women, 33.6; and for Hispanic women, 54.8. One out of four children in the U. S. lives with one parent only; 55 percent of black children live with one parent (Ries, 244–47).

1990, 57.5 percent of all American women are in the labor force, as compared to 76.1 percent of men. While women's labor force participation has risen dramatically since **1950**, men's participation has slowly dropped, due primarily to deindustrialization. Married women are almost as likely to be employed as single women; more than half of all married women with children under six are in the work force (Ries, 306).

1990, four out of five clerical workers are women; around 42 percent of their supervisors are men, as compared to 29 percent in **1979**. In **1990**, 92.1 percent of all bookkeepers and auditing and data entry clerks are women, as compared to 80.8 percent in **1970** (9 to 5).

1991, almost 66 percent of married women are working or looking for work, as compared to 46 percent in **1973**. Between **1989** and **1991**, the median hourly wage for women dropped 4 percent, adjusted for inflation (9 to 5).

1992, AT&T introduces the Videophone. Two new phones are promised for release in **1993**: the Smart Phone, equipped with a touch screen for accessing banking and other services, and the Personal Communicator, a wireless phone that can recognize handwriting and send and receive faxes and e-mail (Ramirez).

2000, an estimated 66 million women are expected to be working in the U. S., accounting for at least 3 out of 5 new workers in the next decade (9 to 5).